Antonio Triana and the Spanish Dance

Choreography and Dance Studies

A series of books edited by Robert P. Cohan, C.B.E.

Please see the back of this book for other titles in the Choreography and Dance Studies series.

Antonio Triana and the Spanish Dance
A Personal Recollection

Rita Vega de Triana

University of Texas at El Paso, USA

harwood academic publishers

Australia · China · France · Germany · India · Japan · Luxembourg · Malaysia · The Netherlands · Russia · Singapore · Switzerland · Thailand · United Kingdom · United States

First published 1993
Second printing 1995

3 Boulevard Royal
L-2449 Luxembourg

Library of Congress Cataloging-in-Publication Data

Vega de Triana, Rita, 1934–
    Antonio Triana and the Spanish dance : a personal recollection / Rita Vega de Triana.
      p. cm. – (Choreography and dance studies : v. 6)
    Includes bibliographical references (p.) and index.
    ISBN 3–7186–5407–5. (bound) ISBN 3–7186–5408–3 (pbk.)
    1. Triana, Antonio, 1906–1989. 2. Dancers – Spain – Biography.
    3. Flamenco. I. Title. II. Series.
    GV1785.T73V44 1993
    792.8′028′092 – dc20
    [B]   93–19472
                                              CIP

For our children, Antonio II and Felipa

ACKNOWLEDGMENTS

This book could not have been completed without the help of my editor, to whom I am indebted for her encyclopedic knowledge and poetic insight – Joan Quarm.

My deepest gratitude to Robert Robertson for his integrity and guidance.

I want to express my appreciation to Donn E. Pohren, for inspiration and information; to Dr. Theodore S. Beardsley, Jr., Director of the *Hispanic Society of America*, who encouraged me to persevere; and to Professors Noeline and Brian Kelly at the University of Texas in El Paso, for their support and unwavering friendship.

To every thing there is a season, and a time to every
purpose ... a time to work, and a time to laugh, a time to
mourn, and a time to dance ....

Excerpt from "Ecclesiastes," Chapter III

CONTENTS

PART I

PART II

INTRODUCTION TO THE SERIES

Choreography and Dance Studies is a book series of special interest to dancers, dance teachers and choreographers. Focusing on dance composition, its techniques and training, the series will also cover the relationship of choreography to other components of dance performance such as music, lighting and training of dancers.

In addition, *Choreography and Dance Studies* will seek to publish new works and provide translations of works not previously published in English, as well as publish reprints of currently unavailable books of outstanding value to the dance community.

Robert P. Cohan

FOREWORD

The first impression of Antonio Triana was brightness.

A small lean lithe man, he swept into El Paso like a meteor, for a retirement which was no retirement, and proceeded to build Spanish dance on the Mexican-American border. If genius is creative energy, he had it in abundance, for he was never still, never without new ideas and plans for performance, never quiet or dull or bored.

Antonio Triana's classes were as exciting as any stage show. In a Latin environment here, he built a troupe of student dancers as good as any professionals, and better than most. When they appeared in concert, the theater was full of enthusiasts from both sides of the International Bridge. Once, when Antonio himself danced, the excitement was almost unbearable.

Until at the end strength failed him, the man was ageless. He had a quality of joy in living which extended to little things and was contagious. Every meeting was a grand reunion. Every conversation was lit with laughter. A dinner party became a fiesta of Spanish food, Spanish wines, Spanish-fractured English, and always the accompanying rhythmic clap of the hands and staccato beat of heels ready to break into dance. There was, as he himself once said, more flamenco in Antonio Triana's kitchen than anywhere.

Certainly, he had cause for rejoicing, both in his achievement and in his devoted family. Rita, the young wife who wrote this book, is herself a gifted dancer and teacher. She was a perfect partner for genius. Both of the children have inherited their parents' warmth and talents. It has been a constant pleasure to count them friends, and a privilege to be associated in a small way with this biography, written in deep love and understanding of the man, his work, and the Spanish dance. I have learned much from the Trianas, including respect for a difficult art form, and I am grateful.

Joan Quarm
El Paso, Texas

PART I

ANTONIO TRIANA

Antonio Triana and Pilar López
Oil Painting by Carlos Ruano Llopis

CHAPTER I

It is said that the "Sevillano" is born with "gracia" – the ability to live life gracefully. For life is a rhythm, a continuous beat, broken only by the stillness which is eternity. Men are born to create or destroy. Most of them accomplish a little of each. Antonio Triana was born to dance, in the city of Seville, the birthplace of the painters Velásquez, Murillo, Valdés Leal; the poets Rioja, Bécquer and Medrano; and the emperors Trajan and Hadrian.

The Romans conquered Hispalis (Seville) in 205 BC, and the city became completely Romanized, as did the rest of Baetica – one of the three Roman provinces into which Spain was divided. The Moorish era that followed was one of splendor, for with it came the building of the Alcázar and the Giralda, the minaret of the great Mosque, built in 1184.

In 1248 King Ferdinand II reconquered the city from the Moors and ruled there until he died. The Emperor Charles V was married in the great cathedral which now houses the tomb of Christopher Columbus and the Archivo de Indias. This contains the most important collection in the world of documents relating to the discovery and colonization of the Americas.

The province of Seville lies in the southwest of Spain near the Atlantic coast, and is divided into four naturally defined regions. The Sierra of the north is a mining zone, with pasture land dotted with evergreen oak trees. The Aljarafe is the fertile plain seen from the Giralda, rich in precious vineyards and olive groves. The Campiña is an area of important villages and large estates. Finally, the Marisma is the marshland pasture preserved for centuries for the fierce fighting animals of the Maestranza, or bullring.

Antonio Triana's father, Jerónimo García Pedraja, came to Seville from the gypsy quarter across the river. A veil of secrecy surrounded his birth, and his children chose to believe allusions to legends of the "cante jondo," the deep flamenco chants of forbidden love and family loyalties. Jerónimo was raised as the only child of Juana and Manuel, but it was hinted that Juana's sister, Carmen, had once loved a gypsy singer of such brilliance that he was awarded the Golden Key of Song for his renditions. Carmen was forced to give their son to Juana, who could bear no children. Indeed, it was whispered that Jerónimo's early education in the seminary was arranged to dispel the stigma attached to his birth. He was to have been a priest, but in his last year of theological study he fell in love with a young Andalucian girl from Écija. His parents humbly accepted his decision to abandon his career, and he married the sixteen-year-old Felipa Matos Pérez that same year. They had four children: Carmen, Rosario (who died

3

in infancy), Manuel, and Antonio, the youngest. It was said that Jerónimo named his daughter Carmen to honor his real mother.

Antonio never confronted his father with these suppositions, for the children of Andalucia kept their places. They studied their parents' moods and reacted accordingly, and so the romantic shadow over Antonio's heritage was never confirmed or denied. It was noted, however, that Jerónimo was irresistibly drawn to "La Cava" where the gypsies lived and practiced their mysticisms.

It was his custom, too, to carry five céntimos coins known as "una perra chica" for the beggars on the bridge linking Triana and Seville, (which the gypsies called "Serba la Barí."). His own favorite story was of the time when he decided to give away an outgrown suit, and invited a relative of the eccentric gypsy dancer, Juan Tumba, to his house to try it on. It was declared "perfecto," and Jerónimo added the vest to seal the bargain. The gypsy was quick to reply, "Dáme cinco duros y no me des el chaleco." ("Give me five duros and keep the vest.") The gypsy code readily allowed selling back a gift.

Jerónimo loved a joke, but when he sang "La Nana," a lullaby to comfort a child, his resonant voice would break and his eyes would fill with tears:

Ese niño chiquito
(This little boy)
no tiene cuna.
(has no crib.)
Tu pare carpintero.
(Your father is a carpenter.)
Te va a hacer una . . . .
(He will make one for you . . . .)

The family shuttled back and forth between Seville and Triana. Triana ... where houses are whitewashed and the white lime stands out in deep contrast against the blue of the sky. Triana ... notorious for its history of gypsies and smuggling. Triana ... humming with street noises, the melancholy concert of sounds of everyday existence.

Here the "pregoneros," or street vendors, sang and recited verses generations old, which boasted of their wares. And here the young Antonio joined the chorus of bread, fruit and broom peddlers, yelling his "¡Cambio cosas!" ("I trade things!") He carried a cardboard tray held in place by a firmly-knotted string around his neck. On it, he proudly displayed his treasures: tin soldiers, horns, even old fuses were all to be sold or traded for toy drums or sweets. And sometimes a youth from the richer section of the neighborhood would be magnificently inveigled into relinquishing a bicycle for something of considerably less value.

This, then, is the Andalucian child: slight of frame, with dark hair and eyes – but the eyes are not those of a child. They are piercing and thoughtful with the knowledge of the ages, for it is the nature of the Andaluz to bear pain without a name, and to yearn without words. Deep within him flows the blood of the conquering Moor, in his heart lies the unerring faith of Moses, and his soul is that of the Arab trader.

April was all excitement in Seville, for then the Feria, or fair, took place, as it still does each year. Warm days and nights were orgies of lights and colors, silks and perfumes, white mantillas and red carnations. The scent of roses and acacia mixed with that of the Manzanilla sherry from the vineyards of Sanlúcar de Barrameda. In little booths called casetas, built for the fair, the dance called "Sevillanas" reigned everywhere. Castanets with dangling ribbons and ball fringe chattered in the dancers' hands. The ruffles of their skirts unfolded like magnolia petals as they moved to the vibrating chords of the guitar.

The casetas were concessions, too, offering candies and "pestiños" made of almonds and honey, as well as seafood from La Isla and Cádiz, prizes and contests. A popular ring-toss game displayed gleaming bottles of a pungent brandy called Aguardiente de Cazalla.

On one occasion a small boy crossed the fragrant meadow of San Sebastián and entered the fairground. He had practiced since the year before with a homemade contraption of pole and washer until he had perfected a certain thrust of the wrist which invariably snared the bottleneck. He easily won five, then six, seven and eight bottles for men of his barrio, until the cheering crowd finally dispersed. Next day, however, when Antonio returned with all his skill intact, the merchant, grumbling about dwindling profits, quickly pulled down the awning and closed his stall. "Se acabó la pesca," he cried. "The fishing has ended."

Song and dance are ever-present in Spain. In Seville, the chant has religious

Antonio's parents: Jerónimo García Pedraja and Felipa Matos Pérez

significance as it moans and trembles with every step of the suffering Christ in the slow sorrowful procession of Semana Santa (Holy Week). More often, on the cobblestone streets, the melodious guitars tell the joy of friendly faces, familiar smells, the union of love, the baptism of a child.

Each "copla" of Andalucian folklore is a poem in itself, and the verses, like Portuguese fados, are sad. The writers' names are lost to time, but the words express sentiments which continue from generation to generation. They will only die if the very essence of humanity is somehow transformed:

> *No te fiés del hombre*
> (Don't trust any man)
> *De mí el primero;*
> (Me, first of all;)
> *Esto te digo, niña,*
> (This I tell you, girl,)
> *porque te quiero.*
> (because I love you).

> *Quisiera verte y no verte.*
> (I would want to see you and not see you.)
> *Quisiera hablarte y no hablarte.*
> (I would want to talk to you and not talk to you.)
> *Quisiera no conocerte*
> (I would want not to know you)
> *para poder olvidarte*
> (in order to be able to forget you).

> *El día que tú naciste*
> (The day you were born)
> *cayó un pedazo de cielo.*
> (a piece of the sky fell.)
> *Hasta que tú no mueras,*
> (Until you die,)
> *no se tapa el agujero.*
> (the hole will not be covered.)

A lament sung from a balcony ... the reflection of the sun on the glaze of ancient tiles as it bathed the Giralda Tower in its rays ... hiding in the deserted ruins of the city of Itálica ... rescuing a half-drowned cat trapped during a summer rainstorm in a medieval drainpipe on the Calle de la Pimienta ... running through the labyrinth of narrow winding streets ... loitering in the bustling marketplaces of La Macarena, San Bernardo and Santa Cruz. ... These are the echoes of childhood engraved upon memory forever.

Then there was the girl. Conchita was ten the year Antonio turned eight. Every day she left her house on Calle San Vicente and proceeded to a very special destination.

Antonio would secretly follow her. He was attracted by the colorful dress Conchita's mother had sewn for this unusual excursion, and also by the enchanting swing of young hips. The boy followed cautiously, darting in and out of doorways until at last Conchita disappeared into a vine-covered patio. He would then approach to read the posted sign: "No Boys Admitted!"

One day, Antonio's curiosity emboldened him to such a degree that he dared to climb up the iron grillework and peer into a window. And there she was! With her were other girls in similar homemade ruffled skirts, and they were dancing! They whirled, played their castanets, and made music with their feet.

Every day for weeks Antonio returned to his secret hiding place, until one day an impatient voice shouted up to him: "My child, if you are going to haunt my school, please come inside and do it!" The great Maestro Manuel Otero had noticed the boy on several occasions, and was intrigued by his persistence and daring. Perhaps the child would be persistent enough to learn, daring enough to perform. Otero had long been searching for a lad of sufficient talent to partner his more advanced pupils. And so Antonio joined the class—not driven by the artistic motives one might suspect, but in order to stand next to the beautiful Conchita.

From the very beginning he showed amazing ability. At eight and nine years old he was creating his own dances. He had an extraordinary sense of rhythm, timing and temperament, and an inherent theatrical insight. He improvised, and he never fumbled.

No one can be taught to perform. The ability to hold an audience cannot be driven into child or adult for money. Otero never even tried. He taught a basic technique of heelwork and castanets which he called "Bailes típicos, andaluces y clásicos." That was all.

Anxious mothers were not even permitted to watch, for, after all, Otero was dancing instructor to the Infantas—the royal princesses, who were not above learning the "Sevillanas." Antonio always had deep respect for his only teacher. He was to mourn years later, when the Maestro was killed by a common burglar.

Antonio's first partner was Otero's favorite, the precocious Francisca Gonzalez, aged twelve. She was called "Quica," then and later, and the children became known as "Pareja de Bailes en Miniatura," or the "Miniature Dancing Pair." They made their debut in a program starring La Argentinita, at the Salon Imperial in Seville, and also performed at fairs and fiestas in the neighboring towns of Carmona, Utrera and Coria.

In 1919 a thin parchment of a playbill from the Teatro de Verano announced three important debuts: the folk singer, Mari Díaz, who was the sister of the brave bull-fighter Pacorro; the cantaor José Rodriguez, or "Niño Medina," and the flamenco artist Antoñito García. His reputation as a child prodigy was rapidly spreading throughout Seville.

It was not unusual for a local impresario to inquire, "¿Cómo se llama ese niño de Triana?" ("What is his name, that kid from Triana?") It was customary, too, for flamenco entertainers to take the names of their town or district as stage names. And so Antonio became Antonio de Triana.

"¡Qué tiempos aquéllos!" he would remember. "What times they were!" The special atmosphere of the café-cantante, "Café Novedades," is lost forever. It was there that La Malena, La Fernanda, La Sordita, Malenita, El Tiznao—the excellent singer from Cádiz,

Playbill – 1919, Teatro de Verano, Seville

and that oracle of the guitar, Javier Molina, held forth. The great ones of flamenco performed nightly, shining in their magic circle of luminous art.

Fandangos
En La Cala hay una fiesta.
(In Cala there is a fiesta.)

Mi mare me va a yeva.
(My mother is going to take me.)
Cuando me vean tan compuesta,
(When they see me so dressed up,)
Me sacarán a baila . . . .
(They will take me out to dance . . .)
¡Olé!

The owner of the Café Novedades approached Antonio's father with an offer of a weekly salary far higher than Jerónimo's own, and so it was decided that the boy would appear there. His career had begun.

La Malena was in fierce competition with one Juana Vargas, who danced as La Macarrona in the Cuadro Flamenco of the Café Kursaal. In fact, both were intense artists, eminently musical, and capable of transcendent performances. La Malena, whose full name was Malena Seda Loreto, was noted for her noble stance. She was a gypsy from Jerez de la Frontera, and her every movement spoke of superb style, control and rhythm. Then there was Juana Valencia, also of Jerez, called La Sordita because she was nearly totally deaf. This was of little consequence, for she never lost a beat of the rhythm or "compás" of the flamenco fiesta. Completing the trio of gifted dancers from Jerez was the beautiful blonde gypsy Fernanda Antúnez, whose stage name was simply La Fernanda.

"¡Gracia y salero!" are figures of speech in Andalucia that express sensibilities, but in any language they are not enough. It is impossible to describe a dancer in words alone. Photographs help a little, but the dancer does not have the immortality of the painter, writer, or composer. His art does not live after him. It is, therefore, useless to try to explain how he would perform a specific step. The flamenco dancers mentioned here achieved a greatness, for they all created their own particular styles and dynamics, which were pure and very personal. They led the young Trianero into their world and he learned and absorbed from the musical forces around him. Like the others, Antonio was born with the elusive gift of soul called "duende." And when it enters the spirit of the dance, the result is art. It is a quality that is indefinable, and it is loved and remembered best.

The hours of twilight in Seville rejoice or sadden the heart. Tangled gardens of geraniums, jasmine, and the budding citrus blossoms called "azahar" smile or sigh behind mute rejas or grillework guarding the Moorish patios. In spring, the life of the city is garlanded with roses.

On May 16, 1920, the streetlamps, as always, were lit at dusk. The fourteen-year-old Antonio arrived at Café Novedades ready to dance, carrying his freshly-ironed white ruffled shirt, or camisolín. But the atmosphere that night was strangely hushed until a distraught Malena beckoned to him from the shadows of the dressing room: "Antoñito!" she cried in a hoarse voice, "¡ha muerto Joselito El Gallo!" The matador Joselito was dead.

The following is an excerpt from an article by José Díaz de Quijano in *La Fiesta Brava* of Barcelona:

Antonio Triana and his childhood partner, La Quica

Dark page. The greatest drama of the arena. Tragic night, the 16th of May. There are no newspapers on Sunday. In spite of the lack of news the brutal rumor invaded the city: the incredible rumor that poured like a tidal wave through the streets and rose like a black cloud over the houses. Joselito killed by a bull!

In the very same Plaza of Talavera de la Reina which had been dedicated by his father, Fernando Gómez (El Gallo I), Joselito had slipped in mud and been gored to death.

In a few days, Antonio would join the weeping caravan of gypsies as they bore their "gitanillo" in an open coffin through the streets of Seville. In the cemetery where Joselito was laid to rest, the sculptor Mariano Benlliure created in bronze a monument of the sad tableau of townspeople, silent and motionless in their grief. The head of Joselito is in white marble.

Joselito, or José Gómez Ortega, had experience, elegance and intelligence in bullfighting far beyond his years, for the Ortega family was steeped in Andalucian tradition. His relatives included the matadors Fernando and Rafael Ortega (Gallo II), the singer El Planeta, who was a gypsy blacksmith in Triana; Ignacio Ezpleta, the flamenco cantaor from Cádiz; and Joselito's mother, who was herself a dancer of the café cantante.

Bullfighting and dancing.... It is not just that these Sevillanos learned about them from childhood. That would have made them only aficionados or enthusiasts. Rhythm and inspirations were in their very souls, and their bodies were perfect instruments to produce the admirable sonority so much acclaimed in their time. They were the very incarnations of mystery, excitement and trepidation.

The legendary bullfighter Juan Belmonte García was born in Triana, in 1892, and from all accounts was reared in Seville's Asilo, or orphan asylum. At the age of sixteen he had made a bare living selling sewing thread on the streets, but his meager earnings could not save him from the ravages of malnutrition. A vitamin D deficiency caused him to be hunchbacked and spindly-legged, and to walk pigeon-toed all his life. This did not prevent his nightly ventures across the river, to tease the huge bulls grazing in the marshland, using a homemade capa.

One Sunday, Juan threw himself into the Maestranza Bullring, and the crowd's shouts of "¡Fuera!" ("Out with him!") quickly changed to "¡Olé!" and "¡Fenómeno!" The startling rhythm of Belmonte's "verónicas" and his manipulation of cloth and stick in the "faena" of the final phases of the bullfight ushered in a golden age of the art. His style blended humility, courage, and tradition.

"¡Cuidado!" his banderillero, Antonio Fuentes, would whisper as a bull sauntered onto the sand. "¡Cuidado, Juanito, éste sabe Latin!" To say that he knew Latin was high compliment to a volatile charging bull. Antonio Fuentes was soon to become related to Antonio's sister Carmen, when she married into his illustrious family. Bullfighting and Flamenco were never far apart.

Juan Belmonte never forgot his humble beginnings. His first action on becoming rich was to buy a house and release his younger brothers and sisters from the orphanage. Nor was he unaware of the fickleness of popularity. In his introduction to *La Escuela de Tauromaquia de Sevilla*. (*The School of Bullfighting of Seville*), he wrote, "Se ve que Pedro Romero mató 5,600 toros y al final de su vida vivió de una pensión de nueve reales diarios." He remembered that the great Pedro Romero, who had killed 5,600 bulls, ended his life on a pension of nine little coins daily, each worth only twenty-five cents. It is not poverty or hunger which forms an artist. It is more likely the depth of his compassion. Antonio Triana, like Juan Belmonte, had that depth.

In all the Plazas de Toros of the Hispanic world, on Sunday at five in the afternoon, matadors march in their suits of lights with magenta capes of raw silk draped over one raised shoulder and one foot toeing in to the other. Their bearing is a deliberate and studied imitation, a grand gesture of respect and homage to the valiant Trianero, Juan Belmonte.

On special religious holidays in Seville the orphans of the asylum were paraded through the streets. They marched and sang, as Juan must have done, their thin hands holding wax candles high. Mothers would tearfully clutch their children to their sides, while others vainly searched the small blank faces, looking for one of their own "mistakes."

The boy Antonio, sensitive to all the stifled emotion around him, would silently vow to earn many pesetas and one day care for all the unwanted ones. It was a child's foolish wish, perhaps, but such are the dreams which move people to gamble with their lives. Unselfish ambition overpowers all fear of change and chance. Matador and dancer shared that quality.

The flick of a fan. . . . The years pass, and tomorrow is suddenly yesterday. The café flamenco, the café cantante which is the "duende," or spirit of the Spanish dance, is dying. La Macarrona says "¡Qué pocos estamos quedando!" "How few of us are left!"

By the 1920s the finest dancers of the era had long been exploited and exhausted. Francisco León, "Frasquillo," had been one of the most virile and vital performers of the old school. He had married La Quica, Antonio's childhood partner, and he was a shoemaker by trade. Late at night, he practiced his intricate footwork on the wooden tops of the trains in the deserted railroad yard of his hometown, Viso del Alcor. Now he danced in cafés, where the salary of six pesetas was far from adequate. Spain had little tourism. There were schools, but the teachers had grown old, and the dancers copied one another. Techniques degenerated into mere mannerisms and memories of past glories. Choreography was stale. There were no new names, and no encouragement to inspire the dimming lights. Dance in Spain was in a state of decadence. Standards fell, until what little occurred was presented in the burlesque theatre, where nude performers wearily shook their castanets. Many a year was to pass before the dance was to be exalted to the Ballet Español.

Antonio was at a crossroads. His artistic ability was obvious, but people no longer treasured their national dances and few performers were rewarded by loyalty or high regard. Furthermore, the boy's father saw theatrical life as insecure and not the work for a man. Aviation was reaching a new frontier in Spain, and so Antonio was sent to Madrid to embark on a career in aeronautics. After several attempts at piloting the flimsy biplanes of the Spanish Air Force, however, he returned to Seville, determined to find work closer to the ground.

Jerónimo, disappointed in his son's apparent failure to conform, now found him a job stoking coal in the foundry Casa Palacios, where he himself was foreman. It was not Antonio's first taste of manual labor, for he had been apprenticed at the age of eleven to the supervisor of the lathe in the Fábrica de San Clemente. Among laborers, he established contact with undeveloped talents lost to the world. Among them were possible Michelangelos, Rafaels, and Donatellos: poets, actors, and musicians who were born too early or too late. They gave their lives to drudgery, for their responsibilities at home were great. They had no time to discover their abilities or desires, and so must live and die unnoticed.

They could talk, though, and over shared lunches of tortillas and oranges, Antonio

La Malena (Malena Seda Loreto), Dancer – Café Novedades, Seville

heard conversations seasoned with the "refranes" or proverbs of their folk wisdom. Refranes contain wit, humor and satire, and are rich in metaphor. They express moral values and feelings, and stress the importance of the individual. Each is a short lesson in integrity, philosophy, and experience, and if it is good enough, it spreads from province to province.

The sayings were popular in Seville, influenced to a degree by the gypsy culture there. Gypsies tend to intensify and stylize truths, and their folk belief, unlike the Islamic faith in absolute destiny, conceives of deliberate human action causing deliberate result. They perpetuate cabalistic signs of mystic rites and ancient aversions to reptiles and scorpions. They have been known to "echar mal de ojo," or cast an evil eye, and the refran "En martes, ni te cases ni te embarques" ("On Tuesday do not marry or travel") typifies their superstition about auspicious days.

No one can contradict the common sense of some of these sayings, born of spontaneous improvisation, for they say much in little:

> *Para el buen entendedor, con pocas palabras basta.*
> (For one who understands, few words suffice.)
> *El que a hierro mata, a hierro muere.*
> (He who lives by the sword will die by the sword.)

Amor con amor se paga.
(Love gives back love.)
Del dicho al hecho, hay mucho trecho.
(It is easier to talk than to act.)
Más vale malo por conocido que bueno por conocer.
(Better the evil you know than the good you don't.)
De tal palo, tal astilla.
(As is the wood, so is the splinter.)

In the foundry, Antonio worked next to a gentle man called "El Sifón" because he sprayed bystanders with his every word, and "El Pelu" (short for peluca – "the wig"), whose shaggy head of curls set him apart from all the others. Like refranes, "motes," or nicknames, are part of daily speech in Andalucia. If one is deaf, lame, or deranged, he is called "El Sordo," "El Cojo," or "El Loco." Rather than ignore a handicap or an advantage, the Andalucian sense of humor emphasizes it. Perhaps this custom reflects admiration for those who despite all obstacles manage to survive. It is surely a concept which accepts both imperfection and beauty with nonchalance, as if to say, "We are not the same, but we are equal."

Antonio danced in the local shows and his efforts were well received, but he knew in his heart that he needed to escape from a future of perpetual "juergas" or flamenco parties. It was a dreary time for the flamencos, wandering from café to café along the Alameda de Hércules. It was a period of nostalgia and memory, for with little to offer from the present, their minds constantly turned to the past. Their fame was fleeting. . . .

The gypsy poet, Cayetano Villanueva, put it best in his Andalucian-gypsy slang called "Caló," when he wrote of the fate of "La Gamba" – The Shrimp, an excellent bailaora who spent her later years in the taverns, sadly recalling her golden days. The poem begins, "Cuando juite marabiya der tablao" ("When you were the marvel of the stage") and ends, "Hoy te encuentras ruinosa dando tumbos po la bia yecha una puri achacosa arrastrá por bajo biento como una estampa borrosa del año mir ochoziento" ("Today you find yourself in ruins, staggering through life as an old withered hag, dragging through time like a faded print of the year 1800").

Artists are often defeated by their own talents, but Antonio wanted to master his dance and not let it master him. He knew that he would have to leave Spain to move on and find his way. Accordingly, he entered the awesome Torre del Oro which housed official government offices, and put his papers in order. He had signed on as cabin boy aboard a freighter, in order to pay his passage to America. He was eighteen.

CHAPTER II

After an eventful, frightening crossing on a half-crippled Spanish vessel, Antonio arrived in New York City. America!

The sounds were deafening, the lights blinding, the crowds ruthless. Walking through the streets, the boy was cold and lonely. But there was the overwhelming sensation of speed, the mechanical industrial marvels which foretold the changing times and progress he was seeking. He knew he must stay in this New World.

The immigrants of the 1920s deserve as much credit for being the Founding Fathers of America as the original pilgrims some three hundred years before them, in the sense that they gave protection and courage to newcomers. They would embrace the foreigner, often giving him food and lodging and, what was more important, conversation with encouragement. New York meant sophistication, Broadway and Times Square, but also neighborhoods where street signs went unnoticed and a stranger knew where he was by the cooking odors seeping out of tenement windows.

As if by instinct, Antonio was lucky enough to find himself in the Spanish Quarter near Roosevelt Street. Juan, the barber there, was from Málaga, and when Antonio walked into his shop asking directions in the familiar Andalucian dialect, Juan closed his eyes and remembered. He listened to the eager boy, studied the determined eyes, and gave the immigrant his first home in America.

Antonio's possessions were few. He was wearing his father's suit. A couple of pairs of carefully darned socks bulged in his hip pocket. His dancing shoes doubled for walking. His castanets went hidden under his armpits. Opportunity, however, was not long in coming. One day an announcement in a Spanish-language newspaper caught Juan's attention. A well-known Spanish dancer from Seville called Maria Montero was to be guest at a banquet honoring the Spanish Consul. The public could attend for a three-dollar admission charge.

The old suit was pressed, the dancing shoes polished, and, armed with his entry fee and a not-too-confident smile, Antonio entered the banquet hall. Juan was convinced that here, somehow, was his prodigy's chance. The dinner itself was auspicious, for those present included Miguel Fleta, Spanish tenor of the Metropolitan Opera House; the famous basso, Mardoñes, and another well-known singer, Andrés de Segurola; as well as Ignacio Zuloaga, one of the few painters who found fame in his lifetime.

There were the usual Spanish toasts and jovial talk of the Old Country, and there was music. Seizing the moment, Antonio invited the Señorita Montero to dance the "Sevillanas." Laughingly, she accepted, but humor turned to amazement as he matched her every step. When the coplas ended she asked him to meet with her to discuss an upcoming tour. She was looking for a partner.

Juan was not surprised when the excited Antonio related all this to him that night. The long-suffering suit was pressed again, and when its owner returned next day there was a signed contract resting in its worn inner pocket. There was also an advance in salary, and the boy lost no time in acquiring an "American" wardrobe. Quickly, he had photographs taken of his new splendor, to send home to his parents in Seville, who had been so certain that their adventure-seeking son would meet only hardship and loneliness, that they had made him promise to return on the freighter which brought him. Now it was long overdue. They were overjoyed to hear from Antonio, and their worry was not unfounded, for the *Cabovillano* had sunk on its homeward voyage, with all hands lost.

In 1925 vaudeville meant three performances a day. Maria Montero was a headliner, booked up and down the circuit. Greasepaint was removed only for sleeping. Antonio slept on lumpy mattresses in odd hotel rooms and walked about the strange cities between shows, buying picture postcards. At mealtimes, after much hesitation, he would point to the first item on the menu and nod to the impatient waiter: "I take thees." After a time he was sure that the whole United States subsisted on filet of sole.

Vaudeville had come to mean a series of unrelated theatrical acts: singers, clog dancers, animals, following one after another in rapid succession. The most famous magician of the day was Harry Houdini, closely rivalled by the illusionist Harry Blackstone, who appeared on the same bill as Antonio. Watching his performances from the wings, Antonio learned the card tricks which he would perform years later for family and friends. His hands flew as fast as his feet. At the same time he learned to speak English from the comics on the program.

He also saw how Prohibition affected them. The song-and-dance men, the acrobats, the jugglers, people who in normal circumstances would never be tempted, carried hip flasks and used them to consume huge quantities of venomous mixtures. Antonio learned to avoid the "carteristas," too, who worked the trains. On occasion, a well-dressed gentleman would "accidentally" bump into a fellow passenger. Hurried whispered talks with the conductor would follow, then frantic useless hunts for wallets which never reappeared.

When they arrived in Chicago the dancers had traveled all night and were tired, but the theatre manager asked to see a dress rehearsal. Antonio was invariably called "El Chico," or "El Niño" (The Little One), and because of this he did his best to mature. In every performance he raised himself high on his heels, and now, at this important rehearsal, he danced with what he thought was a most serious and adult expression. The impresario, who had seen the act and been enthusiastic, was now disappointed. What was wrong? Ah.... He went to speak to Señorita Montero, who in turn conveyed the message to Antonio:

"Ríete, niño, o estamos en la calle." ("Smile, boy, or we'll be out in the street.")

It was his boyish smile, his uninhibited dancing, free from slick mannerisms and tricks that set Antonio apart. He was not "a Spanish dancer," but rather a Spanish boy, dancing.

At this time the superb Spanish singer Amalia Molina had a large following in the vaudeville circuit. Her troupe included the well-known Spanish tenor Manuel Alda and a dancer from Aragón known as "Palitos." His specialty was the "Jota," which he performed well, but Amalia, herself from Seville, wanted to present the Spanish dance in its most exciting form, which to her was that of Andalucia.

She sent her personal manager to catch the Montero act and have a look at the young dancer from Triana. The man reported back in superlatives, and within a week they made him an offer. This was a flattering proposition, but also a lesson in humility. Antonio felt guilty leaving Maria Montero on such short notice, and even worse for costing a fellow countryman his job. But it was such temptation! Here was the chance of a fifty-week tour on the famous Keith-Albee Circuit, with a raise in salary. Soon they would appear at the Palace, and a banner headline would proclaim:

Palace to Present Great Star Today
So Spanish is the dash and fire of her dancing that one leading writer called her "The Soul of Spain." Amalia Molina is today considered one of the very foremost artists that Europe has sent to the stage of America. This very personification of terpsichorean grace, as seen in the alluring dances of Spain, is the very happy selection as a headline attraction of the new bill coming to the big theater today. Assisting the beautiful artist are Triana and Alda, a clever team of her countrymen.

When an act played the Palace Theatre in the heart of New York's theatre district, at Broadway and 47th, it had reached the pinnacle of success, as part of the most powerful vaudeville chain in the nation.

Antonio signed a contract without business advisors or a personal manager. He put his trust in the judgment of the older and wiser, being barely able to read English and understand the small, or, for that matter the big print on the document. He was given his costume, a shoddy garment trimmed with a few battered sequins, and advised that part of his salary would be withheld until it was paid for. Long after that costume had been worn to shreds the boy was still paying fifty dollars a week for it. Exploitation, yes, but he was young enough to take it and more. His success overshadowed his doubts, and so he danced.

He danced until he was tired: tired of the "three-a-day," tired of the makeup which wouldn't always wash off, and most of all, tired of receiving only half of his salary. In Dallas, Texas, he bade "Adiós" to Señora Molina and with the money he had managed to save, boarded a train for California. Los Angeles, Santa Barbara, San Diego—the Spanish names intrigued him and drew him to what was indeed once considered a New Spain.

And there was something more: Hollywood, the Mecca of the silent pictures. Charlie Chaplin was the idol of millions of fans, and there were rumors of "sound," for *The Jazz Singer*, starring Al Jolson, had been filmed by the Warner Company. "Talkies?" Just a novelty.

Rudolph Valentino died in 1926. Apart from setting female hearts afire, he had accomplished a remarkable thing. This actor, with his sensitive dark looks, whose sensuous Tango had so rapidly replaced the Charleston, had made American audiences aware of the Latin. The Spaniards, French, and Italians were no longer the mustachioed villains: they were now the leading men and heroes of the "flicks."

Hollywood then was only a few streets lined with the eucalyptus and palm trees of another era. Antonio walked up Hollywood Boulevard to Gower Street and saw a sign, "Rooms to Let." This was a streak of luck, for adjacent to the boarding house was a dance studio, where for fifty cents Antonio could rent a large space and practice for an hour or more. In no time he acquired an audience of fascinated spectators, who soon were begging for lessons.

For five dollars an hour, Triana took on several pupils of Spanish dance, and after much demand, taught a bit of the Argentinian Tango. After one of these lessons, a pupil remarked that there was to be an important audition for Tango dancers, which Antonio should certainly attend. Sid Grauman had recently opened his Chinese Theatre with the silent movie, *The King of Kings*. With it he presented an elaborate stage show which had proved an inspirational spiritual experience. Now it was decided that the newly completed film *The Gaucho*, starring Douglas Fairbanks, would premiere at Grauman's. The accompanying program would draw its theme from the movie.

Twenty-four couples, all proficient Tango dancers, with appropriate experience and costumes, were already waiting to audition when Triana and his partner reached the theatre. At last their turn came, and they climbed the steps leading to the huge stage, and faced the dark cavernous auditorium. In that blackness sat Sid Grauman and Douglas Fairbanks, and when *The Gaucho* opened, Antonio Triana was the featured dancer.

What sort of Tango did he dance? Surely not the trite routine of a patent-leathered-hair gaucho with a bored partner. Here were strength and authority, a Tango more reminiscent of Cádiz than of Buenos Aires. The spurs on his boots became his castanets, in a symphony of crackling sharp exotic sounds. It was a triumph.

That night, Charlie Chaplin went backstage to visit his friend Johnny Puleo, the diminutive harmonica player known as the "Argentine Rascal." Chaplin paused to congratulate Antonio, who was awed and speechless, almost....

"Your derby," he said. "May I try on your derby"

"Take it. It's yours," replied Mr. Chaplin.

Dolores del Rio also stopped by, to invite Antonio to dance the Tango with her at the opening of the Hollywood-Roosevelt Hotel. The host of this grand gala was the irrepressible American humorist, Will Rogers.

Another visitor, Gus Edwards, a producer for Metro, signed Triana to appear in the first musical "short" made in sound and color. It was *La Mexicana*, in which Antonio was to perform his now-celebrated Tango, together with a Spanish "Garrotín." There was talk of more films, contracts, and scripts.

But the talk faded. In his dancing, Triana was commanding and aggressive, but in close-up on film he was what he was—shy, slim, handsome and young. The head of the studio decided that he would arouse women's maternal instincts rather than their romantic interest. His boyishness and foreign accent were obstacles not easily overcome.

Antonio was disillusioned, and there was no one to console him, to remind him that he was unique and not easily molded to the standard Hollywood pattern. He took inventory of himself. He had achieved success and money, but it was early spring. Soon there would be Feria in Seville.

Then came a final blow. Someone stole Charlie Chaplin's derby from his room in the boarding house. It was time to go home.

CHAPTER III

The booming sounds of cities were left behind now, and it was a relief to hear the muted bells of distant conventos, and to sit in shaded courtyards, watching soft lights flickering through treetops and iron grilles. But Triana was not left in idle peace for long. The technicolor short he had made at Metro was being shown at a movie theatre in Seville. Incredible – that a Sevillano was the star of an American film! An impresario, in a propitious move, sought out Antonio at his home in Triana and persuaded him to appear at the Teatro del Duque with the most successful revue company in Seville. Since his appearances coincided with the showing of his film at another theatre, he became a local celebrity.

This was the start of a curious sequence of events in Antonio's artistic life. Destiny had prepared coincidences, accidental meetings, a series of fortunate circumstances which would provide the opportunities to show and prove his talent. His success was not to be the work of fate alone, though, for he responded to each new challenge with amazing ability.

By this time, Antonio had created a very special repertory for himself. He was not limited to Spanish dances because their appeal to Spaniards was small. Instead, he performed what the people wanted to see: the dances of other countries, quick polished routines in the fast new foreign rhythms they had only heard about.

And for an encore he would peel off his smoking jacket, be joined by a guitarist, and dance flamenco. The word was a mere memory to his genteel audiences, but Antonio had never forgotten and his dance awakened something inside them, too. Once again it became their dance, their sound, their heritage. They screamed "¡Olé!" Triana was a sensation. He was heralded as Bailarín and Bailaor; that is, equally adept in the classical and flamenco techniques. He was the supreme male dancer.

After a lengthy engagement at the Teatro del Duque, Antonio went to Madrid for a much-needed vacation, but there he was urged to perform at the Teatro Avenida, and spotted by Juan Carcellé. This producer was involved with a new form of entertainment in European nightclubs, where singers and dancers were conducting orchestras. Carcellé, much impressed by the young Triana, signed him to conduct and dance with an outstanding group of musicians, some of whom would later be known as "Los Churumbeles de España" ("The Little Gypsies of Spain"). Triana was fast acquiring fame in Madrid, and before long he was introduced to Eulogio Velasco.

Velasco was surely the Ziegfeld of Spain, a man of discriminating theatrical taste and acumen, for after World War I he had presented Spanish Dance in New York for what was perhaps the first time, with a program starring Antonio Bilbao and La Argentina. He managed the largest and most successful revue company in Madrid and he saw in Triana not only an exciting performer, but the makings of an excellent choreographer. He was forced to wait, however, as Antonio was already contracted by Manolo Sugrañes and his revue company for the following season. He was scheduled to appear with Raquel Meller, who had starred in 1926 in the first European film of *Carmen.*

Raquel Meller, born in Aragón in 1888, was known as "El Alma Que Canta," or "The Soul that Sings." She was a major attraction in Spain in the early years of this century, and appeared at the Empire Theatre in New York in 1926. It was said that she had a peculiar genius, a hypnotic and alluring singing style which took Spanish music halls by storm.

Before he was to work with her, however, Antonio was approached by the father of a young dancer about to make her debut in Madrid at the Lido Club. She danced only flamenco and had taken some lessons from Frasquillo and La Tanguera. It was hoped that Triana would teach the girl numbers to be performed with orchestra as well as guitar. He began with his choreography of "Claveles Rojos" ("Red Carnations"), with music by his brother Manolo, a fast-rising composer.

The girl responded admirably to Antonio's coaching, and in rehearsals her father saw them as an ideal team. He was intent on joining the two, and so it was at the Casino de la Perla in San Sebastián that Antonio Triana and Carmen Amaya danced together for the first time. Their paths soon separated, however, for Carmen went on tour in the provinces and Antonio headed towards Barcelona and the Sugrañes Company.

Antonio and his brother shared genes of talent and temperament. Growing up in Seville, Manuel, or Manolo, had acquired vast knowledge of all flamenco's moods. His first love, however, was the piano. As a child he studied organ with the eminent musicologist, Padre Eduardo Torres, at the Catedral de Sevilla, where the boy demonstrated unusual gifts of musicality and harmony. Manolo became the solo oboeist with the original Orquesta Bética de Cámara, established by Manuel de Falla. These musicians were the proud descendants of the glorious Iberian composers. In their programs, past met present, including works by the modernists Stravinsky, Shostakovitch and Schoenberg.

Manolo worked in close collaboration with Falla for more than a decade and forged artistic ties with the other protégés, Ernesto and Rodolfo Halffter. After all, their mothers had played together as children in the neighboring village of Écija. Ernesto was conductor of the Orquesta Bética, and, after his mentor's death, completed Falla's "L'Atlántida." Rodolfo in later years was to direct the Triana-choreographed production of *El Amor Brujo* at the Palacio de Bellas Artes in Mexico City.

Antonio's brother also dabbled in classical composition, giving new expression to folklore themes from Asturias, Luarca and Aragón. He developed the unique ability to play flamenco guitar rhythms on the piano, empowering them with his own "duende" or profound emotion. He originated a new instrumentation for traditional authentic musical forms.

Manolo accompanied Antonio on many of his dancing tours, and for his brother's class routines he composed "Castiza," "Farruca Jerezana" and "Seguiriya Gitana," all inspired by nuances of the guitar. Furthermore, he arranged and orchestrated original songs for

Anita Sevilla, Mikaela, and the flamenca Lola Flores. He wrote "Canasteros de Triana" for Antonio and Rosario, who were known as "Los Chavalillos de España" ("The Kids from Spain").

Carmen Amaya sang and danced his Zambras, "Véte Con Los Tuyos" and "La Tana," with its compelling lyrics:

> *Mi mare se llamó Tana*
> (My mother was called Tana)
> *desde la pila de su bautismo.*
> (from the time she was baptized.)
> *Y yo por nacer gitana*
> (And because I was born a gypsy)
> *el pare cura me puso lo mismo.*
> (the priest named me the same.)
> *Al compás, de palillos y guitarra*
> (To the rhythm of castanets and guitar)
> *a éste mundo vine yo....*
> (into this world I came....)

Manolo used his mother's name professionally, and when he died in Alcalá de Guadaira in 1988, Manuel García Matos was one of Andalucia's most respected composers.

Back in the 1930s, as now, an important aspect of life in Madrid was the sidewalk café. Miguel de Unamuno, Spain's intellectual giant, poet and essayist, frequently declared that Spanish culture was to be found more in the cafés than in the universities. Here were the conference tables. While sipping aromatic Cuban coffee, negotiations and promises were made, contracts were signed. Men plotted and planned their politics, their plumbing, and their poetry.

A chance meeting with Eulogio Velasco at such a café, after Antonio's return from Barcelona, led to a new direction in his career. After some polite conversation, Velasco, the master showman, offered Triana the position of choreographer and leading dancer with his revue company, whose permanent address was the Teatro Reina Victoria. Velasco's revues were considered spectacular and bold. He hired the finest actors and singers in Spain. The most beautiful showgirls were in his choruses. Costumes and scenery, mostly imported from Paris and New York, were breathtaking.

Triana's versatility enabled him to create ballets and adapt them successfully to the theme of each show. One, called "Cabaret Nights," ran for a year in Madrid. Antonio staged some fifteen other productions, among them *Morena y Sevillana*, a musical comedy in which he danced with Julia Verdiales. He met her husband, Antonio de Bilbao, who was an important figure in the dance world. He was born in Seville, but as a young child was taken to Bilbao, where he was raised in a non-Andalucian environment. From his photographs we can see that he was a short chubby man, far from the conception of the male Spanish dancer, who is a slender, glowering tiger. But Antonio Bilbao was astounding.

He first performed at the Café de Columnas in Bilbao, and later made his debut in

Sevilla at a café cantante. His small booted feet would mount a round wooden table and, accompanied by the guitarist Luis Molina, fire off a sharply accented "Zapateado." His heelwork was a wonder, for then, in 1925, the male dancers had not yet developed any formal technique, and their steps were comparatively simple.

Despite rumors to the contrary, and in spite of those who claim to be the heirs of his "school," it is a fact that Antonio Bilbao never taught anyone his "baile." Not even his own son! He once told Triana, "Yo no enseño ni a mi padre." ("I would not teach my own father.") "And if my son will dance, he will struggle as I did, working out the difficult and complex 'taconeo' [heelwork] by himself. If I were to make him a gift of it, he would neither appreciate nor respect it." A wise man.

Antonio Bilbao did not teach Antonio Triana. They admired and deferred to each other's talent, and while they drank coffee together, Bilbao spoke of his dance. He gestured and indicated, and from these clues alone Triana was able to add to his own technique and further develop his own "sello," or trademark.

The legendary La Argentinita (Encarnación López) was born in Buenos Aires. Her parents, Felix López and Dominga Júlvez were of Castilian extraction, and the family returned to Spain, where a second daughter, Pilar, was born in San Sebastián. As children, the sisters performed the regional dances and Encarnación, or Encarna, schooled herself in the arts of pantomime and singing. She enjoyed success imitating the temperamental Zarzuela singers famous during her youth, and later joined an acting group founded by the prolific playwright Martínez Sierra. His *El Reino de Dios* (*The Kingdom of God*) served to open the Ethel Barrymore Theater in New York in 1928.

Encarna's scintillating personality endeared her to the intellectuals of Madrid. Her friends included Jacinto Benavente, the Nobel Prize-winning playwright, Ernesto Halffter, and Ignacio Sánchez-Mejiás, the bullfighter who was to influence her career. She worked in close collaboration with her friend Federico García Lorca, Spain's great musician-poet. Together they explored and collected folk material of the provinces, and both were drawn to the flamenco art, the pulsating rhythms of Andalucia.

In 1933, La Argentinita decided to dance *El Amor Brujo*, a ballet by Manuel de Falla. It is the story of two gypsy lovers, Candelas and Carmelo, who are kept apart by a sinister apparition or spectre, until at last the promise of life and redemption triumphs over death.

Argentinita and Ignacio Sánchez Mejías, who had agreed to sponsor the presentation, contracted the Orquesta Bética de Sevilla, and so intent was Encarna on creating an authentic "gitano" atmosphere for the ballet that she engaged the flamenca bailaoras, La Malena, La Macarrona, and La Fernanda to perfom with her. She arrived in Seville with Pilar to start rehearsals. Her search for a male partner, however, was proving unsuccessful.

The oboeist of the Orquesta Bética heard of her predicament, and now he intervened: "There is only one dancer in all of Spain who can interpret the role of Carmelo. He is my brother, Antonio Triana."

"He was the boy who appeared with us in Novedades. He can dance anything!" cried La Malena. Argentinita dispatched a telegram to Madrid at once.

Manuel de Falla's one-act puppet entertainment called "El Retablo de Maese Pedro" won first prize in Madrid's Academy of Fine Arts in 1904. In 1905, Falla composed an opera, *La Vida Breve*. He managed to go to France and he remained there to study for seven years. His dream was to have *La Vida Breve* produced on the stage, and it was presented in Nice in 1913. Falla taught music in Paris and became intimate with Ravel, Debussy and Dukas, returning finally to Spain, where he settled in Granada. In 1914, Falla and the dramatist Gregorio Martínez Sierra were asked by the gypsy dancer Pastora Imperio to compose a work in which she could both sing and dance. The result was the ballet-pantomime, *El Amor Brujo*. The first performances fell short of expectations, and in revision, Falla added the role of the gypsy girl, Lucía. Since then *El Amor Brujo* has gained critical acceptance. The Ritual Fire Dance is perhaps his most popular composition. As a dancing score the ballet begins well enough, but there is the danger that the dramatic action may falter after the Fire Dance. It is only when the ballet is performed by actor-dancer-artists that its emotional force can be sustained.

The Sociedad Sevillana de Conciertos of the Teatro San Fernando in Seville, a branch of a cultural organization which put on plays in major cities of Spain, gave Falla the opportunity to establish his Orquesta Bética de Cámara.

As a small boy, the composer had visited Seville with his parents, and he had been inspired by its torrent of rhythms ever after. It was fitting that the rehearsals of *El Amor Brujo* were to take place there.

Argentinita, Antonio Triana and Pilar López, as Lucía, began to create their dances. The finished choreography was achieved through a mingling of their ideas and improvisations.

There was a triumphant opening night at the Teatro Falla in Cádiz, followed by a complete tour of Spain. The company also offered "Conciertos de Danzas," in which they performed the works of Turina, Bretón, Albéniz and Granados. This was the birth of the Ballet Español as we know it today, and the association of Triana, Argentinita and Pilar López was the start of mutual artistic admiration which lasted for many years, although Antonio rejoined the Velasco Company in Madrid at the end of the tour.

"Paris and Madrid—jealous of Barcelona, which had the good fortune to see the *Amor Brujo* at the Liceo Theatre, for there shone the impetuous hurricane force of Antonio Triana."

So read a prominent critic's impression of another presentation, this time in 1934, in Barcelona. An impresario had contacted Falla, who was living there at the time, and proposed a performance of *El Amor Brujo* and *La Vida Breve* with Laura de Santelmo as ballerina and choreographer. Falla had seen the woman dance and did not think her strong enough to choreograph so major a work. He replied that he would only consent if Antonio Triana did the choreography and performed in the opera as well. Tempers flared, but Santelmo relented and rehearsals began.

Laura de Santelmo was an enigma in the Spanish dance world. Her work showed moments of solemn poetry and inspiration. Her hands and arms were as graceful as birds, but she had a flighty temperament. She surprised theatre managers by demanding her full salary just minutes before curtain time. She was, to say the least, disruptive. Now, she refused to perform the dances of *La Vida Breve*, and four soubrettes had to be imported from Madrid, along with Miguel de Molina, who was to dance the role of

Carmelo. Antonio had decided to choreograph the part of the malevolent Spectre for himself. Molina was later to become a famous and prosperous singer in South America, but he arrived in Barcelona unprepared and had to borrow Triana's "chaqueta corta" for the show. To his consternation, the jacket was too short and his shirt sleeves were visible....

The impresario, Mestres, in his desire to create authenticity, put out a call to all the flamenco dancers in Barcelona to gather for an audition. Antonio met old friends, the gypsy sisters called Las Hermanas Coquinera, and Rafaela Valverde. Rafaela, known as La Tanguera, was more goddess than sorceress in her role as La Bruja, for Triana remembered her as an Aphrodite of the dance. Her arms, footwork, and expressions together manifested untold of burdens and joys.

Juan Lamote de Grignon led the Orquesta Sinfónica de Barcelona, which he had founded, for *El Amor Brujo,* and Falla conducted *La Vida Breve.* It was a historic program, for this was Falla's last public appearance in Spain. The critical Barcelona audience was deeply moved by the majestic foreboding of *El Amor Brujo* and to Santelmo's astonishment, the dances of *La Vida Breve* were an unqualified success. Falla was delighted, and congratulated Triana. La Laura immediately called a rehearsal for next day, announcing that she would replace the girls in the dances.

The Madrileñas went berserk. They followed Santelmo back to her elegant hotel on the Plaza de Cataluña. With murder veiled by beaded eyelashes, they accosted her in the dining room. Antonio could only speculate just how they convinced her to stay out of their danzas, but the issue was settled the following morning when Falla annnounced that there would be no program changes.

Four performances at the Liceo were followed by a tour of Catalonia, after which Triana returned again to Velasco in Madrid. It was during this period that he gave lessons to prominent dancers and singers of the day, including Conchita Piquer, with whom he appeared at the Teatro Zarzuela; Pepita Embil, who was to become the mother of Plácido Domingo; Charito Leonís, Reyes Castizo (La Yanqui) and Conchita Leonardo.

CHAPTER IV

The Spanish Civil War of 1936–39 was fought with great valor, much bitterness, and horrible destruction to both sides. It will never be possible to determine accurate figures for the deaths from bombings, battles, political oppression and disease. In addition, thousands went into exile. Every part of the country showed the wounds and horrors of war. It is estimated that fewer Spaniards were executed by the Inquisition in over three hundred years than were murdered in Madrid in the first three months of the Civil War.

Junkers aircraft, fighter squadrons and Messerschmitts supplied by Hitler played a vital role in bombing attacks. At his Nuremberg trial in 1946, Herman Goering admitted that he had advised Hitler, in what was to be his first international move, to help Franco. It was "to test my young Luftwaffe," he said.

No democratic nation sent military officers or advisors to help the Spanish Republic. All the foreigners fighting were volunteers whose governments disavowed their existence. The single reason for the victory of Generalissimo Franco and the Nationalists was German intervention, for the Condor Legion with its tanks and artillery proved to be the most effective fighting force on either side. It became obvious that the Fascists were using Spain as a testing ground for their global expansionist techniques. It was General Hugo Von Sperrle, Commander of the Condor Legion, who masterminded the bombing of Guernica. Pablo Picasso's great painting, *Guernica*, was inspired by the ruthless bombing of the defenseless town.

Madrid in 1936 was pitiable. Civilians were worse off than the soldiers, dying of starvation and pestilence. Electricity was rationed. There were long food lines for the short supplies available. Dogs and cats disappeared. Rats were sold for food in the Plaza Mayor. The banks closed and Antonio traded lessons for bread and cheese. He huddled among the Madrileños in the underground metro stations, to be warm and safe from bombs.

García Lorca's prediction had come true: "Las lágrimas amordazan al viento; y no se oye otra cosa que el llanto. . . ." ("Tears muffle the wind, and nothing is heard but the weeping. . . .")

Since the future of theatre was now bleak, many artists migrated to Paris. Triana was contracted to perform in Nice, and left for Barcelona once more, this time to obtain a visa and proceed to France.

The dynamism of inspiration that is inherent in a liberal democracy would now be blocked in any future that the artists could discern. They refused to take part in benefit

"El Amor Brujo" – Teatro Liceo, Barcelona
Standing – left to right: Miguel de Molina (Carmelo), Manuel de Falla (Composer), Laura de Santelmo (Candelas), J. Lamote de Grignon (Conductor), Antonio Triana (as Spectre and Choreographer)

programs profiting the Fascist order of things. Dance had formerly contributed enormously to the Spanish Theatre, but now many of the finest talents were dispersed.

Carmen Amaya and her cohort of gypsy guitarists, singers and dancers, sensing the impending upheaval, had boarded a ship heading for Portugal. Antonio's brother, Manuel, was the company's pianist and advisor. Armed with hastily assembled costumes, the group descended on a Lisbon café.

"No gypsies, ever!" yelled the exasperated manager.

"Tonight we dance for free," countered Carmen, "but tomorrow ... a cóqui!"

And pay up they did, for next evening a line of customers worked its way around the city block, as word of the frenetic performance, touched as it was by the pathos of the forced exile from "La Madre Patria," spread throughout the city. A month's contract was assured. Only later, in Argentina, were they to meet with Antonio again.

"Oh, lost people in the Andalucia of tears...." So wrote García Lorca. In 1936, he was shot and killed, not far from the site of his greatest inspiration, the Alhambra in Granada.

A despondent Argentinita made her way to Paris, alone. She had also lost her beloved Ignacio Sánchez Mejías who met death on the estribo in 1934, passing a bull of the fierce

Guisando strain. He was immortalized in his friend Lorca's "Lamento." Pilar López was dancing in North Africa. Antonio Triana was teaching in a small studio in the Montmartre district of Paris, unaware that Encarna was rehearsing alone in a hotel basement nearby.

She had agreed to let Marcel de Varmalette sponsor her in a solo recital at the Salle Pleyel Theatre, but although as creative and vibrant as ever, she was not at heart a soloist. Argentinita believed that the purpose of the dance was to convey both masculine and feminine attitudes. She wanted excitement high on both sides of the footlights, for in order to fully interpret characterization or thought, she felt that communication between performers was essential. Technique was merely the instrument for projecting dramatic effect. In a solo situation she could not be artistically content. She sought out the reactions of cleaning women and janitors during rehearsals, convinced that the humble people were more perceptive than the critics.

Sidewalk cafés on the Rue de la Paix and Étoile now substituted for those of the Gran Viá and Las Ramblas. The Spaniards sat there in their self-imposed exile, pondering their destinies and from time to time twisting their verbs in an attempt to learn the French language. Among them was Pablo Picasso, who invited Antonio to pose. Sadly, Antonio could never find the time, for an hour sitting meant one hundred francs lost teaching. Life was too insecure.

Pupils are as distinct as fingerprints. Each offers a challenge to his master. The discovery of a major talent and its development is the ultimate accomplishment. But in theatre, rules are often broken. Mediocrity may achieve unqualified success while genius is left by the wayside. The very sensitivity which forms the artist can often destroy the determination and aggressiveness essential to achievement. A teacher, then, aside from possessing technical aptitude and competence to pass on his craft, must have the insight of a trained psychiatrist.

If talent was conspicuously non-existent, Triana always found it less cruel to discourage rather than build a pupil's false hopes. When the dancer, Vicente Escudero, asked him to teach his only son, Antonio was faced with this very dilemma. After a few lessons, in all honesty, he suggested to Vicente that the boy should seek a career in another field.

As years pass, the dance teacher becomes an indisputable judge of character, but at times even intuition fails. Antonio had such an experience while working in Paris. Señor Pacheco, who owned the studio where he taught, introduced him to a prospective pupil. At first glance, Antonio decided that the girl would be ideally suited for life in a cloistered French convent. Her hair was severely pulled back from a plain face devoid of makeup. Her clothes were dark and drab. Triana could not understand why anyone so obviously shy and withdrawn could consider a theatrical career. Spanish dancing, he explained to her gently, was a most free uninhibited form of movement, perhaps not quite what she was seeking. But the girl was adamant about learning, and as time went on, Antonio had to admit that she was quick and had acquired a lofty grace, even in her tight stiff collar and long, restricting skirts.

Then one evening a friend invited Antonio to the celebrated Folies Bergère. It was a rollicking show of beautiful, scantily clad women. The finale was a Venusian bacchanale, where a large shell was moved onto the stage and from its pearly depths

"Danza del Terror"—*El Amor Brujo*, Antonio Triana and Laura de Santelmo
At lower left: La Tanguera, Las Hermanas Coquinera

arose the star attraction: a magnificent creature, completely nude. She waltzed across the stage to tumultuous applause, soft light shimmering over her perfect body. Antonio stared in bewilderment, for he had recognized his timid pupil. Convent, indeed!

The girl arrived promptly for her lesson next day, but Antonio never revealed his discovery and she continued her charade until he left France. He was not to trust his instinct again for some time.

News finally spread to Argentinita that Antonio was near. She rushed to his studio in Place Guelma, confident that by once again combining forces the Ballet Español would survive "even the revolution." She was too late. Triana had just signed a contract to go to Budapest. He took Argentinita to dine at the Moulin Rouge, where they applauded the Spanish dancer, Goyita Herrero, but after champagne at the Chez Pizarro, Antonio was obliged to hurry back to his small apartment to pack.

He found the Danube River dividing the twin cities of Buda and Pest oddly reminiscent of the Guadalquivir which parts Seville and Triana. But a far cry from the Caló gypsy still fresh in his memory were the tribes of Romany gypsies who had somehow made their way into Hungary. The "palmas" and "cante jondo" were born by the shores of the Mediterranean, but these gitanos were small boys haunting the coffee houses with quivering violins for the few coins tossed their way.

Spanish dance can cross all boundaries of understanding, and Triana's audiences loved him. They were particularly impressed by his "Fire Dance," and the owner of the Café

La Argentinita, Antonio Triana, Pilar López, in the classical "Panaderos"

Ostende implored him to extend his engagement. Pre-war Hungary was lively and carefree, for only close to the German border was there any hint of the terror to come to all Europe as World War II. Yet Antonio was anxious to return to Paris, for he had received the following telegram from Argentinita:

INDISPENSABLE LLEGUE – OCHO NUMEROS NEUVOS – ENCARNA.

(Imperative – you arrive – eight new numbers.)

Still, the Hungarian authorities held his papers. "Agree to stay longer," threatened the Café Ostende, "or no passport!" Through the ages performers have struggled for their artistry, and now Triana was being blackmailed because of it. The destiny of the Ballet Español would have to wait yet another two weeks.

Rehearsals began immediately when Antonio did return to Paris. Pilar had arrived from Tangier with her husband, Tomás Riós, and the guitarist Manolo de Huelva had joined the company. The brilliant composer, Manuel Infante, was their pianist. Argentinita had decided to stage his "Danza Gitana."

She envisioned an Andalucian street scene: A lovely señorita realizes that she is being followed by a dashing caballero. She spurns his advances. He reasons that the pursuit is not worth the effort and stomps away. The girl dances alone, repenting her hasty morality. To her delight, the man returns, enfolds her in his voluminous cape, and the two leave the scene together.

The execution of this dance to the rhythm of "Bulerías" involved far more inspiration than perspiration. More pantomime than dance, it was an exercise of split-second timing between Argentinita, Triana, and the score. Each gesture was exquisite in taste and in detail. An entrancing, lighthearted profile of the Spanish ego, it was listed on the program as "El Piropo"—"The Compliment."

Every dance conceived for the Salle Pleyel concert was not only representative of Spanish rhythm, but also of Spanish thought and manner. The Parisian audiences and critics had never seen such a perfect combination of subtlety, style and strength. Once in a lifetime can we find dancers able to translate and transmit the mood of the sultry café or the provincial feast to the concert idiom. This, La Argentinita, Antonio and Pilar managed to accomplish. They were consummate artists who, by shrug or nod, told a tale of intrigue or mirth.

CHAPTER V

The Salle Pleyel concert led to contracts to perform in Marseilles, Monte Carlo, Biarritz and the French Riviera. It was during a return engagement at the Pleyel that the impresario Sol Hurok was in the audience. He had seen Argentinita some eight years earlier in New York, during the Lew Leslie International Show, but her art was lost in that gaudy revue. She was, after all, a delicate porcelain. When set in a cheap frame her colors were distorted. Light and shadow lost substance. Such was the initial presentation of Argentinita in New York, and it is of interest to note that the musical comedy star, Gertrude Lawrence, and the ballet dancer, Anton Dolin, were part of that same unfortunate program.

It left such bad memories that Argentinita was reluctant to try again, but Hurok convinced her that the trio would make dance history. They, who had shown Spanish dancing to Spain, would now set out to conquer the Americas. Their guitarist of the moment, the renowned Ramón Montoya, sadly enough, would no longer be with them and would never reach America. Surrendering to his own gypsy fear of migrating long distances over water, he refused to travel farther.

For the most part, American audiences had only a vague notion of what Spanish dancing should be. In the past there had been so few Spanish attractions of any merit that the audiences had no standards by which to form opinion. It was a revelation to them to see Spanish dancing by native performers, for it is and always was impossible to imitate or in any way approximate the fundamental characteristics of the art.

In this case, authenticity was unquestionable. Indeed, theatrical effect would often be sacrificed for its sake. Internal energy inspired the dances, in comparison with false external exuberance which only too often replaces it.

Comparison between Argentinita and another Spanish dancer was inevitable. Antonia Mercé, whose stage name was La Argentina, had been born in Buenos Aires when her Spanish parents were on a dance tour of South America. Her father was premier danseur of the Madrid Opera. Her mother was the premiere danseuse, and this was the position little Antonia herself assumed at the age of eleven.

She had the advantage of early individual training from her Castilian father, who was a teacher of the Bolero school, but the routines of classical ballet did not satisfy her. She went on to master the works of Albéniz, Granados and Falla, and her choreography was entirely her own. It revived and at the same time revitalized the folk art of ancient Iberia.

La Argentina first appeared in New York in 1918, but her earliest major triumph was a solo concert in Paris, which she repeated in New York's Town Hall in 1928. She toured America the following year and returned almost every season until her death in 1936. John Martin, the distinguished *New York Times* critic, wrote of her: "To rank Argentina as second to Anna Pavlova is to make an insidious comparison, for she is second to none in her individual way...."

Argentina possessed the wiles of a fashionable woman, and her dance was described as sparkling and vivacious. She was often called "Queen of the Castanets," for in her youth she experimented with their shapes and sizes until she created instruments of subtle varied tones which expressed her every shade of emotion. This she accomplished with four pieces of wood fastened together by a simple cord, which up until her time had been considered merely minor percussive instruments.

On one occasion, Triana was invited to dance with La Argentina in Madrid, but when

Antonio Triana—the gallant suitor of "El Piropo"

it was learned that he had already performed with La Argentinita, the association became unthinkable. Yet, in retrospect, the careers of the two women were complementary, rather than competitive. Both were highly capable of transforming rhythm and phrasing into physical form. Both were warm and gracious, and their art was beautifully conceived and performed.

Elated with the success of their New York debut, Sol Hurok sent Argentinita's group on tour, and Antonio was jubilant when they reached Los Angeles, for it was a chance for him to visit his old haunts again. He walked the downtown streets, greeting familiar places and missing those which had disappeared in the shifting landscape that is a growing city.

He paused by the huge Central Market. Mediterranean people relish all things which swim or float on the sea. Life without an occasional morsel of squid, prawns or clams would be dull indeed. . . . So, loaded down with an ample supply of raw jumbo shrimp, Antonio returned to his hotel room, well armed for an orgy of fond memories and fish.

After a time, though, he began to feel very sick. He put in a hurried call to George Perpere, who was Hurok's stepson and the current company manager, and announced that he would not be able to dance. The hotel's resident physician was called in and confirmed the verdict. There would be no show that night!

Still refusing to surrender, Perpere deluged Triana with orange juice and aspirin, until at last much of the offending evil was expelled. He half-dragged the dancer to the Philharmonic Auditorium, and at 7:30 Antonio began applying stage makeup to his green-tinged complexion.

And that night Triana danced as never before. . . .

Perhaps it was the combination of a high rising fever and the soaring intensity of his own artistic nature, but he literally burned up the stage with a demonic energy. His feverish state was obviously contagious, for he was persuaded to encore one number after another. At the end of the performance, the audience called on him to speak:

"All this," he gasped, "on aspirins and orange juice!"

The backstage dressing room was mobbed with aficionados and old friends. Here and there a stranger would pump Triana's hand effusively, and earnestly confess, "I knew your father, the Tango dancer."

Argentinita, Antonio and Pilar knew the value of genuine, rather than simulated informality. In their dance, they were all poise, dignity and restraint, and there was considerable skill in the building of the program. Tradition sparkled with humanity, and the magnificence of the small company was its simplicity of understatement. Only when artistry is soundly grounded can it appear effortless. Much "went over the American heads," to be sure, but the following season these dancers were to find a reception in the United States unsurpassed by any others.

On their return to Paris at the end of this engagement, the trio began to rehearse a new repertory. They were not inclined merely to coast on their success, and refused to allow their interpretations to become hackneyed by repetition. Their "Jota Castellana" was a frequently encored number, but it was inconceivable for them to repeat it on a second tour. Creativity was not a chore to them: it was their calling and their way of life.

Many recitalists suffer from the disadvantage of being their own choreographers. To devise and arrange a composition of steps and then perform it apparently requires a

La Argentinita, Antonio Triana, Pilar López, in the original "Jota Castellana"

stronger musical-philosophical bond than the average dancer possesses. Triana actually liked the process, as well as the fruits of it. He had the intangible power. His grasp was instant, his recall phenomenal, and with his uncommon kind of equilibrium, he was able to establish a riveting choreographic identity.

A talented Spanish pianist Mercedes Miracles often played for him when he taught and rehearsed his own repertory. One day she handed him a musical score which she had copied by hand, with care and precision. The notes swept over the pages, feathery markings belying the surging strength they indicated. She explained that La Argentina had shown great interest in performing the work, had felt inadequate in her choreography of it, and had sadly abandoned the project. For the first time, Antonio heard the haunting melody of "El Polo," and as he listened, his mind already danced, the musical passage of Isaac Albéniz taking form and motion.

The guitar rhythm "Polo" is derived from the "Siguiriya," as are the "Soleares" and "Martinete." The great Tobalo is credited with first singing the "Polo," and the song is described as "Cante Grande," the true flamenco, dissimilar from the "Malagueñas," "Sevillanas," and other street dances.

In Seville, the "Polo" came into being amid the sounds of the blacksmith's "Tonás" and "Martinete." Like the "Soleares" and "Cañas" it is native to Utrera, Triana and Dos Hermanas. In Cádiz, the "Polo" found place with the "Tango" and the "Alegrías" of Sanlúcar, Chiclana and Arcos de la Frontera. As written by the classical composer, Tomás Bretón, and danced by Pilar and Antonio, it was clearly based on the guitar rhythm "Soleares," and Albéniz was drawn to a similar source while composing his "Polo."

It is astonishing the way people of other nations respond to Spanish arts. They find the folklore of García Lorca and the flamenco fascinating, and it should be remembered that many of the world's most famous composers went to Spain to seek artistic stimulation. Rimsky-Korsakov, Ravel, Debussy, all wandered across the Spanish landscape. Stravinsky wrote "Espagnola" in 1917, after his journey to Madrid. Glinka traveled the Calle de las Sierpes in Seville, attempting to translate and note down graphically all the sounds and rhythms. Falla described Spanish guitar music as being melodically Moorish and harmonically Spanish. It was, and is, totally compelling.

Russian Ballet has often been attracted to exotic Spanish motifs, from the time of Marius Petipa, who, as maitre de ballet of the St. Petersburg branch of the Imperial Russian Ballet, exerted much influence on all classical dance during the late nineteenth century. In 1842, he was invited to perform at the King's Theatre in Madrid, where he remained for four years, producing ballets and acquiring knowledge of Spanish dancing. He was later to compose some fifty-four ballets, many of which, such as *Don Quixote*, must have been prompted by his memories of the bullfighter's pose and the Spanish dance movements.

There was also Colonel Wassily de Basil, who immigrated to Paris after a distinguished military career. He dallied in the arts and eventually became manager of a Russian opera company which featured Chaliapin. De Basil formed an artistic association with the French intellectual, René Blum, and out of their mutual infatuation with the dance, the Ballet Russe de Monte Carlo was born. The company boasted the talented choreographers Fokine, Balanchine and Nijinsky, and enjoyed a prosperous first season at the Champs-Elysées Theatre in Paris.

However, sometime during the fourth year of its existence, an internal struggle took place between the dancer Leonide Massine and the Colonel, which was never to be resolved. Massine, financed by wealthy Americans, and with Serge Denham as executive director, formed a new Ballet Russe. René Blum carried on with his Ballet de Monte Carlo, while De Basil gathered about him the remaining loyal dancers and continued the company under his own independent banner.

During 1938, the Ballet Russe appeared at the Drury Lane Theatre in London, in direct competition with De Basil's company at the nearby Covent Garden. It was at the latter theatre that British audiences first thrilled to Rimsky-Korsakov's elaborate Russian fairy tale, *Coq d'Or*.

That was a year for dance, as the same season, Argentinita, Triana and Pilar were performing in London at the Aldwych Theatre. Listed on the program as Antonio's first solo was the Farruca, or Miller's Dance from Falla's *Three-Cornered Hat*. Ballet dancers swarmed to the theatre, for it was, after all, their first chance to see the "Farruca" performed by a Spaniard.

Diaghilev had first produced *The Three-Cornered Hat* as a ballet in London in 1919. The scenario was by Martínez-Sierra, based on Antonio Alarcón's novel, *El Sombrero de Tres Picos*. The original choreography was classical and balletic in structure. Dancers had been animated by the passion of the music, but no one had been able to perform the "Farruca" with the indomitable spirit of Triana. He danced it as Falla must have visualized it, expressing in his timing and phrasing the authentic Andalucian rhythm which for centuries has been called "Por Farruca." This "Farruca," then, was a fiery emotional display of Triana's energy and skill. It was clearly the high point of the program, and night after night, had to be encored.

The classical ballet dancers went to Triana's dressing room backstage to ask for lessons. Certainly, they did not intend to learn Spanish dancing, but they were sincerely motivated by a desire to bring that same sensuous force into their own work. Yurek Shabelevsky, David Lichine, Yura Lazovsky, and Alberto Alonso met with Triana in the basement of Covent Garden Theatre, where he taught them his "Farruca." At a pound a lesson, the ballet dancers tried to absorb in a few sessions the fervor and profundity of this foreign art form, while a brooding Leonide Massine and a beaming Colonel De Basil sat back and watched with rapt attention.

Triana was perhaps the first Spanish dancer to appear on British television, for the BBC invited him together with the guitarist, Gabriel Ruiz de Galarreta, to appear on the cultural program entitled "Picture Page."

The tour continued. The guitarist, Carlos Montoya, joined the company. Scandinavia rang with "¡Olé's!" and Spanish stomachs grumbled as they reluctantly adjusted to frugal dinners and enormous Dutch breakfasts. The Hague, Schevinengen, Amsterdam, Brussels: and then back to Paris to prepare for a second tour, which was to encompass all the major cities of the United States, Canada, and South America.

A typical evening's program opened with the "Sevilla," danced by Antonio and Pilar. "Sevilla" is from the *Suites of Iberia*, by Isaac Albéniz, who was a pupil of Franz Liszt. Some of Albéniz' music shows the influence of the French Impressionistic School, but the source of his creation was always Spain. He was born in Catalonia, and his *Suite Catalonia* was inspired by the folk music of his native land. It was first performed in Paris in 1899, with the composer conducting, for Albéniz, preferring composition, was a rarely gifted virtuoso. Of his many pianoforte compositions, the finest is a set of twelve pieces entitled *Iberia*, of which Argentinita performed the "Mallorca," "Triana," "Malagueña," "Asturias" (Leyenda), and "Castilla." The solo called "Córdoba" comes from a collection of Albéniz' piano pieces which he named "Chants d'Espagne."

The dances, "Zapateado," performed by Argentinita and Pilar, and "Orgia," danced by Triana and Pilar, were taken from *Danzas Fantásticas*, by Joaquín Turina. "Jota de Alcañiz," danced by Argentinita, and "Farruca Torera," performed by both sisters, were composed by Manuel Font y Anta, a disciple of the Sevillian-born Turina.

Authentic traditions of Spain were also genuinely represented in the musical comedy

Antonio Triana "El Polo"—Essence of the Andalucian gypsy

light operas called "Zarzuelas." These neither copied the style of grand Italian opera, nor the risqué French operetta. They had their own entity. Drawing material from popular tunes, the "Zarzuelas" intermingled the events of ordinary life with elements of human comedy and political intrigue.

"Pan y Toros" (Bread and Bulls) is one of seventy-seven "Zarzuelas" composed by Francisco Barbieri. In it, picturesque nineteenth century Madrid is brought to life, and it was the time of toreros, majos and majas, patriots, beggars and conspirators. The painter, Francisco de Goya, is a main character of the plot. Argentinita chose a page from this major work as her first solo on the program. She incorporated steps from the "Paso-doble" and the "Seguidilla Madrileña" to give the dance a flavor of antiquity.

CHAPTER VI

The Company left Le Havre in France for Argentina in 1939 aboard the Italian liner *Massillia*. They basked in the sunshine and took part with some amusement in the sentimental ritual enacted at the crossing of the Equator. In Buenos Aires, their premiere performance at the Odeon Theatre was attended by the distinguished Spanish author, playwright and journalist, Federico Ramos de Castro. He dashed backstage after the final curtain, and was ushered into La Argentinita's dressing room; but it was Antonio he wanted to see, and the result of a long interview was a stupendous article which appeared in the Argentinian art publication, *Guión*.

Ramos de Castro had none of the abbreviated hurried style of the news reporter. He wrote a stunning portrait of Triana the man, the dancer, and the artist. He described Antonio's dance as being a total of all the man knew and was. Yet it was never Antonio's intention to overshadow Encarna or Pilar. The three complemented each other to a remarkable degree. They threw out sparks of vibrant intensity at each other in every performance, and responded in turn to the intoxicating stimuli. They not only changed costumes between dances: they changed as people, too. Antonio was the only male dancer, and attention was naturally drawn to him. He gallantly courted the sisters onstage, never forgetting for a moment that the Spanish male is the most masculine of dancers.

As the bullfighter dances and mystifies his bull, Antonio, with his invisible cape of magnetism, brought his audiences to a similar frenzy. It is not just by coincidence that "¡Olé!" is shouted at both toreros and Spanish dancers who are found deserving. There is much similarity between matador and dancer; the bravura, the defiance, the arrogant posturing and the serious countenance.

Yet it would be a mistake to infer that one imitates the other. It is more correct to assume that both are forms of Spanish art, aggressive, passionate, and often tragic. The parallel is as emotional as it is physical. The pose and the stance are altogether Spanish. They are personal individual expressions of confidence and pride, rather than theatricality.

It was at this time of promise that Argentinita became ill. The announcement was cause for dismay, and in private moments, Triana assessed how this unforeseen development could change the course of his career. He and Argentinita, together, had explored the frontier of the Spanish dance adventure. The largesse of their achievements would pave the way for dancing generations not yet born. Without their co-creativity, an abyss would remain. . . .

An eminent doctor advised Argentinita to forego her exhausting schedule and submit to immediate surgery. She refused. She would not allow her company to wait idly by while she regained her health. Triana begged her to reconsider. He already had enough pupils in the Argentine capital to keep him occupied until her recovery was complete. But no, the pain was not too great, and she decided to continue. She did agree to take a short rest, during which time Triana and Pilar gave a successful concert at the Teatro Cómico.

"Goyescas," which Pilar danced, was actually the "Intermezzo" from the opera *Goyescas,* by Enrique Granados. He took the name from a collection of piano pieces which were written before the opera and were suggested to the composer by various paintings and etchings of Goya. Granados had gone to America in 1916 for the production of *Goyescas* at the Metropolitan Opera House in New York. He was drowned returning to Europe, when a German submarine torpedoed the *Sussex* in the English Channel.

Like Falla, Granados had been a pupil of Felipe Pedrell. His compositions were the result of a highly developed piano technique, and at one time he transcribed, for piano, some twenty-six unpublished harpsichord pieces by Domenico Scarlatti. Pilar and Antonio performed his "Danza XI" with all the passion and fire Granados must have dreamed of while composing this provocative interlude.

The role of Pilar López in the history of the Ballet Español should never be underestimated. She was an artist with a vital sense of rhythm and line, with the added advantage of being an accomplished pianist. If Triana and Pilar were to lead a company today, their achievements would surely bring about a renaissance of interest in the Spanish dance.

When Argentinita assured everyone that she was on the mend, they continued their journey through the Argentine provinces of La Plata, Córdoba and Rosario, on to Montevideo and finally to Rio de Janeiro, where they boarded the *SS Brazil* and sailed to New York for their opening there. On this second tour of the United States, the small troupe would sweep the continent from coast to coast and add all North America to the lands already worshipping at the shrine of their dance. They demonstrated again and again that although their art was based on Spanish tradition, it projected a fundamental harmony. Their dances were sentimental renderings of their inner vision. Their choreography was balanced and expansive, both emotionally and musically.

The itinerary took them as far north as Vancouver, Edmonton, Manitoba and Calgary. They shivered as they disembarked from trains into arctic temperatures, their smoldering Spanish comments forming puffs of vapor in the frosty air. They were further disconcerted when applause from Canadian audiences was subdued. What a relief to learn that people had worn their furlined gloves and mittens into the chilly theaters!

The company traveled through the Midwest and then the Southwest. By this time, the "Huayno" was added to the repertory. Critics named it "the greatest dance of our generation." It was performed by Argentinita and Pilar to an authentic Peruvian song which expressed faith, dignity, and the Incan stoical acceptance of all things. It was a somber yet wonderful contrast to the flamenco luster, which further proved that pure folk tradition, the sounds from the soul and the roots of a people can be presented in formal classical concert format.

Rogelio Machado, the concert pianist who accompanied the dancers on this tour, was born in Oran, Algiers, of Spanish parents. His exotic environment, centering as it did on Moorish tradition and order, allowed him to develop a precise approach to his music. Together with his polished technique, his intuition and formidable imagination enabled him to interpret and arrange any Spanish thematic material into a dance score. He was an essential member of the group, and he formed a lifelong friendship with Antonio.

In Harlingen, Texas, the Company crossed the border on a train bound for Mexico City. Such travel could become monotonous and they often passed the hours in stimulating conversation. Antonio would also stand on the outside platform of the baggage car, with no companion but the desolate landscape and the occasional screech of the train whistle; and then his feet would beat out counter-rhythms to the steady pattern of the grinding wheels. These impromptu sessions gave him the idea for a new dance creation, a complex, staccato "Zapateado" which he was to set to a violin composition by Pablo de Sarasate.

Triana's goal in choreography was the reconstruction of the authentic Spanish dance: classical, regional and flamenco, freeing all forms from fantasy. He researched Spain's past with the accuracy of an anthropologist, believing that by having a glimpse of history, one could better portray the origin and impulse of his people.

In his studies, Antonio discovered that the ancient Phoenician city of Gadir was once called the City of Dances. It was founded by colonists from Tyre around 1100 BC. It disappeared in time, and now the city of Cádiz stands above it. But when archeologists uncovered the original city, statues of dancers were unearthed. Their formal pose, with

Rogelio Machado, Pianist, Pilar López, Antonio Triana, La Argentinita, Carlos Montoya, Guitarist (nephew of Ramón Montoya) – Buenos Aires, Argentina

perfectly erect torsos, influenced Triana's interpretation of his "Zapateado." The finished dance was poetic in its precise meter and accent, and in its conception Triana had reached the summit of technical virtuosity.

Daniel, the Mexican impresario, had arranged a week of concerts for the Spanish dancers in the Palacio de Bellas Artes of Mexico City. It is an ornate building, an architectural blend of both Mayan and Mixtec cultures. The theater has a curtain of colored glass by Tiffany which depicts the volcanoes Popocatepetl and Ixtaccihuatl. It is used as a backdrop for displays of illumination.

Performances in this glittering setting met with wondrous applause, and newspaper reports were eulogies rather than criticisms. Artistry and excellence were praised and glorified, as the Spanish dance reached a dazzling height of popularity in the Mexican capital. Mexico City, after all, is patterned very much after the cities of Spain. The language, of course, is Spanish and the national spectator sport is the bullfight. Triana felt very much at home there. He always had high regard for the past civilizations of the Toltecs and the Aztecs, and now seized the opportunity to investigate the ruins of their ancient pyramids, palaces and temples.

Unlike his companions, Triana was unaffected by Mexico City's high altitude. The dancers were not able to limit their activities until their systems became accustomed to the thinner air, and as a result, Argentinita and Pilar were not feeling well. Without them, Antonio studied the historical murals of Diego Rivera in the National Palace of the Zócalo, and walked about the "mercados" of San Juan and the Lagunilla, little inconvenienced by the tropical summer rains.

The Catalan sculptor Angel Tarrac, who was living in Chapultepec at the time, cast a statue in bronze of Antonio in a dance pose. The figure is a silent communication of protean energy and intensity. Tarrac is well known for his monument at the large bullfight plaza in Mexico City. His outstanding "Abraham Lincoln" stands as a tribute to the American president in a downtown area of the city of Juárez on the Texas-Mexican border.

When at last the troupe left Mexico on a train heading towards the eastern cities of Philadelphia, Boston and Hartford, Antonio felt a compulsion to return to the beautiful country whenever he would have time to travel its broad plateaus and explore the scenic highlands. He was to go back to Mexico, and sooner than he imagined possible.

The final series of concerts for that season was in New York, as guest artists with the Rochester Philharmonic Orchestra in a symphonic program devoted to the music of Spain. José Iturbi, the musical director, believed that interpretation of the music of his native country would be incomplete without the accompaniment of the vibrant dancing it suggests. The audience reacted with enthusiasm to Argentinita's robust "Jota de Alcañiz," Pilar's lyrical "Goyescas," and the matchless foot rhythms of Triana's "Farruca."

At Carnegie Hall approximately half the program was encored. Critics described the performance as incomparable, and John Martin wrote of Triana, "His 'Zapateado' stopped the show cold last night!"

The songs of the poet, García Lorca, found a special niche on the program. "Café de Chinitas" was an amusing romantic triangle set in a smoky café of old Málaga. The penetrating "Anda Jaleo" told of mountain smugglers in the Sierra Morena.

Argentinita sang them in her direct, clear, silver voice. Mime was artfully woven into the fabric of the dance, and castanets were eloquent and articulate. The Company performed without scenery of any kind, their costumes a myriad of rippling colors and a constant variety of shape and form. Audiences were subjected to ever-changing panoramas, from a cool, stately "Mazurka" of the 1890s to an impetuous "Zambra" in flickering light of glowing embers in a gypsy cave.

The dancers now decided to remain in New York for a much-needed holiday. In the interim, Triana received an invitation of considerable importance. La Paloma Azul, a cultural organization in Mexico City, sponsored by the Ministry of Education, had selected him to stage, choreograph, and perform the *El Amor Brujo* ballet for a special presentation at the Bellas Artes.

Pleased to be returning to Mexico so soon, Triana decided on impulse to travel the long distance by car. It was a hazardous journey, up and down the lofty peaks of Tamazunchale, with unending curves climaxing in steep precipices, for the Mexican highways were not the monitored paved roads of today. And once the shaken Triana

Pilar López, Antonio Triana, La Argentinita, in "Café de Chinitas," by García Lorca

arrived in Mexico City, he was faced with the challenge of finding local dancers who could in a short time respond to the demands of his forceful choreography.

The motion-picture actress Margo had been assigned the role of Candelas. During the time she spent in Hollywood under contract to a major studio, she had given some memorable performances in American films. Fortunately, she had also studied dance with Triana, and was aware of his teaching method and choreographic style.

Emotion was to be stressed in this production. There was deep understanding of the character's feelings, and the result was pure dance-drama. Candela's poignant love for Carmelo was evident, as was her dread of the Spectre, her obsession with the past, and the gypsies' superstitious terror of the spirit world.

In addition to the *Amor Brujo*, they performed *El Piropo*, borrowed from Argentinita, which again utilized Margo's acting skill. In a lighter vein, she danced the "Molinera," the fanciful solo of the Miller's Wife from Falla's *Three-Cornered Hat*. It was a perfect complement to Triana's impassioned "Farruca" from the same score.

The company included Martín Caro, as the Spectre, Anita Sevilla as Lucía, and the gifted Carmen Romero. Rodolfo Halffter conducted the Mexico City Symphony Orchestra.

The success of *El Amor Brujo* led to a clamor for lessons, as usual. Triana's pupils now included Luisillo, Antonio de Córdoba, Rafael de Córdoba, Roberto Iglesias and Manolo Vargas. For a time, Antonio actually intended to remain in Mexico, where he felt a sense of artistic satisfaction and fulfillment. He began to form the nucleus of his own company. But Sol Hurok wrote from New York with alarming news. He asked Antonio to seek out another partner, for it was more and more apparent that Argentinita's health was failing.

CHAPTER VII

Carmen Amaya was appearing at the El Patio nightclub in Mexico City when Antonio wrote to Sol Hurok, praising her singular abilities. Hurok sent a contract back immediately, authorizing him to sign her for an American concert tour. First, however, Amaya had to complete an engagement in Buenos Aires. The impresario planned to see her perform there, as he was traveling with his Ballet Russe on the South American circuit.

Accompanied by the conductor Arturo Toscanini, Hurok first saw Carmen dance at the Teatro Maravilla. Toscanini was amazed by her gypsy temper and torrid rhythms. Both were quick to perceive that Triana and Amaya together would prove an unbeatable combination.

There was then the question of obtaining passports and visas for Carmen's clan, which included performing members of her family, several cousins, an uncle, and a few in-laws. As well as Sabicas (Agustín Castellón), there were guitarists of varying abilities, their manager, of sorts, Domingo Blanco, and, although the Amayas did not own an automobile, there was a chauffeur who could not be left behind. Like all gypsies, the Amayas had strong family ties, and they had always managed to stay together. There were close to fifteen of them on tour. Carmen's parents, Micaela and José, who was called Pepe, or El Chino, looked after all of them.

Born in the gypsy quarter of Somorrostro in Barcelona, Carmen was little more than a child when she began performing in the taverns; her unique aptitude for rhythm and movement already in evidence. Those were grand times in Barcelona, at the Bar del Manquet de Atarazanas, where one could be served fragrant coffee with three sugar cubes for one peseta, and at the same time be entertained by a "Cuadro Flamenco" which included Carmen Amaya, then called "La Capitana," her aunt Juana (La Faraona), La Romerito, El Gato, and the guitarists El Chino (José/Pepe Amaya) and Manolo Buleriás.

Dancing was in Carmen's blood: Her style was unorthodox and her choreography spontaneous. Nearly always improvising, she rarely performed a dance twice the same. This was her appeal, and Triana would make a brilliant partner for her, as he could harness his own bursts of energy at will, and had the additional power of a faultless technique.

In the Spanish cafés, the public is patient. It allows the dancer to warm up. It will forgive an off night, and be willing to return and view the artist when he is "in the mood." And when is he in the mood? In his own relaxed element, and not in a forced setting of canvas scenery and glaring spotlights. The impresario, Diaghilev, once

Antonio at the moment he stepped into the spotlight at Carnegie Hall to dance "Zapateado", by Sarasate

attempted to present the typical "Cuadro Flamenco," but the dancers were out of place in the elite atmosphere of a Parisian theater, and the venture failed.

It now fell to Triana to train the untamed Amayas in concert choreography. Their entire nightclub repertoire lasted only twenty minutes. Gypsy dancers do not easily take instruction from anyone, yet now there was to be the discipline of costume changes, the following of a set program. More important, the spontaneity of their improvisations would have to be channeled. A graduate course in Granados, Albéniz and Falla was now imperative for the Amayas.

Her independent gypsy spirit made Carmen reluctant to admit having to take lessons, but Antonio was one of the few "payos," or non-gypsies her father found trustworthy. He ordered his boisterous children, "Listen to Triana!" And since Pepe was indisputably the boss, they obeyed. Antonio was frequently called into Hurok's office, where the near-desperate impresario would exclaim, "What am I going to do with all those gypsies?"

Finally, in order to feed the numerous Amayas, Hurok arranged to have them perform at the Beachcomber Nightclub, on Broadway. During the twenty-week duration of their contract, Triana worked with them for two hours a day. Behind the locked doors of their penthouse apartment, permanently reeking of sardine, they studied. Antonio taught Carmen his choreography for Albéniz' "Córdoba," the "Fire Dance," from *El Amor Brujo*, "Sacromonte," by Turina, and Infante's "El Piropo." Her sisters, Antonia and Leonor, whose main contribution to the act had been their exacting sharp "palmas," or hand-claps, were taught "Goyescas," a "Farruca de Jerez," and a lively "Jota."

Sol Hurok had his eye on a Carnegie Hall opening, and in spite of the trials and hardships Triana encountered in preparing the wayward company, he assured Hurok that they would be ready. As well as the Amayas, Triana taught a hectic schedule at New York's Galo Studio. It seemed as if all the city were attuned to the Latin beat. The "Rumba" and "Conga" were in vogue, and the Cuban singer, Desi Arnaz, had just begun his drumming to the strains of "Babalú." Manolo Vargas arrived from Mexico City for more advanced training, and from Brooklyn, José Greco joined Triana's ever-increasing roster of students. The subways coming and going out of 7th Avenue were brimming with would-be Spanish dancers.

Triana's authenticity and natural love of rhythm added a depth to his teaching which defied imitation. He generously imbued his pupils with both the "taconeo" (heelwork) and the tradition of his beloved art; and so it is today that practically all American Spanish dancers have been taught directly by Triana, or indirectly by his students. The very shoe they wear was patterned by Mr. Capezio after the first Spanish dancing shoes Antonio took to America.

All the arts boast of marvels and prodigies, and there have been those few Spanish-Flamenco guitarists whose musicianship eclipsed all others. Ramón Montoya, Niño Ricardo, Javier Molina, and Manolo de Huelva were all virtuosi. Triana performed with all of them. Not merely endowed with deft fingers, these musicians had the power to punctuate their strict tempi with flashes of invention and originality. The roll of honor would not be complete without the name of Agustín Castellón, or "Sabicas." He devised infinite variations on a theme. His scope of melodies was inexhaustible, and with the change of a chord, Sabicas could turn a dance into a rhapsodic rendezvous or a raucous jamboree. A large measure of Amaya's success was due to his efforts.

No less than four guitarists were to take part in the Carnegie Hall debut. They were: Sabicas; Carmen's father, Pepe; her brother, Paco, and the gypsy El Pelao. The entire program was under Triana's direction, and he prepared a varied fare, a very mosaic of dance to play up the strengths and camouflage the faults of a company so young in concert experience. Antonio himself added considerable power to the proceedings with his "Polo," which was to receive seven curtain calls from an enthusiastic full house. That night, Triana heeded Hurok's sternly given advice not to encore in an already lengthy program. But when Hurok stormed backstage, inquiring, "Well, why don't you encore?" Triana felt obliged to mutter some choice Spanish expletives....

In their flamenco duets, Carmen was at last able to relate to a partner her equal in unbridled vigor. Not before, or since, was she able to respond to a male dancer with that same animal ferocity. There was always a spirit of challenge between Antonio and Carmen, and the theater fairly melted under the heat of their scorching personalities.

Headlines next day proclaimed, "Carnegie Hall—Set on Fire! Flamenco Performance Leaves Capacity Crowd Limp!"

Encouraged by the reviews, Hurok began booking the company for a tour across the United States. The entire organization was to function because of Triana's perseverance and patience, although an important consideration was Carmen's father's admiration for the American dollar. But, with no trust in banks or other financial institutions, Pepe doled out salaries when the mood struck him. When he did, the gypsies combed the sleazy downtown pawnshops in search of gold earrings and diamond stickpins. The guitarists took to wearing outdated pinstripe suits, silk scarves and loud ties. Thumb-prints and X's began to appear on hotel registers across the nation, and an epidemic of missing towels must be chalked up to the Amaya era.

Still, because of her father's inborn theatrical instincts, Carmen was at her best when he coached from the sidelines. In the middle of his "falseta" guitar melody, Pepe would whisper to her just when she should accelerate her rhythm, and then signal to her when to initiate a break and take a breath.

But he exploited her, took her earnings, and squandered them. "¡Qué se divierte!" she would say, "Let him enjoy himself!" when anyone complained to her about his latest

The Amaya Clan: Antonio Triana and Carmen Amaya
Left: José/Pepe Amaya; Right: Paco Amaya; Background: The Amaya Sisters

spending spree. That would end the matter. Carmen was to remain a dutiful, grateful daughter until the day her father died. She never knew or imagined a gentle, sheltered existence. There was no whimsy in her dance. Her humor was frank and brutal.

Carmen's histrionic "Piropo" with Triana was inevitably greeted with howls of laughter and the number was essential, but it was no secret that she was as subtle as an atom bomb. Triana discovered that by contrast to her tempestuous bursts of song, her sister, Leonor, had the husky plaintive tones of the old Flamenco. Her songs were to add a longing, caressing note to their "cuadro."

Backstage, the atmosphere was generally strained. Antonio would be shouting last-minute instructions to performers and stagehands, in two languages. The Amayas would try to calm their jittery nerves by nibbling on hard-boiled eggs, tomatoes and chocolate bars. And Sabicas would jokingly accompany it all by strumming the entrance to the "Capriccio Espagnol" on two rubber bands fastened to a matchbox.

Eventually, Carmen's eccentric eating habits were to prove her undoing. In Boston, she collapsed at the end of the "Fire Dance," and could not rise with Triana for the bow. (The dance concluded with a series of lightning-fast turns, finishing on the knee.) Fortunately, it ended the first part of the program, and, despite an extended intermission, the audience was unaware that Carmen had to be revived. Only by sheer willpower did she continue the performance.

Carmen was equally at ease dressed as a mischievous boy in tight pants or in her flamboyant gypsy dresses with trailing yards of ruffles. A few agitated movements onstage would have her hair astray and her flowers flying. Once, in Cincinnati, a patron in a front-row seat ran moaning from the theater during Carmen's opening number. Her eye had become the target for one of Amaya's jet-propelled hairpins!

It was a whirlwind tour, culminating in New York, where the troupe entertained the First Lady of the land. Eleanor Roosevelt was so carried away by the excitement that she swept both Triana and Amaya into her arms and lifted them off the dance floor. It was in New York, too, that Triana set a precedent by preparing a series of Sunday afternoon concerts for the Museum of Modern Art. These were called "Coffee Concerts," in deference to the steaming cups of coffee served during intermissions. The innovation attracted both dance and art enthusiasts, for the two are related, and an atmosphere in which both can be enjoyed is ideal.

In Triana's mind, painting and sculpture were ideas and movements captured on canvas or frozen in wood or stone. The dancer is the painter's brush, then, stroking lines and living shapes and drawing lights and shadows. The images of the mind become an iridescent palette.

New York was clearly the hub of theater and all the arts, but Antonio could never feel completely settled amid the turmoil of so large a city. Nor would he become accustomed to the harshness of New York winters. Bundled up, with head held low, he trudged dejectedly through the slush each day to the rehearsal hall. On one occasion, he crashed head-on into a fellow pedestrian, who staggered a bit and groaned, "Mira donde vas, Triana!" "Look where you're going!" With a twitch of his outlandish moustache, Salvador Dali took the encounter in stride and continued to propel himself through the freezing sleet.

Antonio longed for the mellow evenings of a Paris spring. World War II was entering

Guitar Virtuoso—Sabicas

its final stages, however, and it was still impossible to travel abroad. California seemed to hold the answer to his growing restlessness. He had been approached by motion picture studios which had shown great interest in him as dancer and choreographer, and an important Hollywood dance studio was also eager to employ him as teacher. Regretfully, he left the Amayas, who continued to tour.

The young dancer Luisillo, or Luis Dávila, whom Antonio had trained in Mexico City, joined them with his partner, Teresa. He was eventually to head his own company, the Luisillo Ballet Espagnol. His extensive training enabled him to execute "renverse" turns of great velocity in his Spanish dance, and his flamenco style was one of feline grace.

Amaya herself never achieved Argentinita's total immersion in her art. Her upbringing was not one of castles and castanets. As far back as she could remember, there were always hungry people around her, craving her support. All her life, they were to rely on her powerful heels, and she would never let them down.

Carmen was a brewing hurricane, exploding into pounding thunder and battering rain down over a barren land. Just as quickly, the cloudburst would cease, and she would be gone.... The essential Carmen was somewhere else, somewhere you couldn't follow....

CHAPTER VIII

In his travels, Antonio had become something of an art collector. He had found time to attend art auctions and sales in the cities along his route, his purchases being classics and the Spanish masters. In California, he would be free to pursue his hobby by browsing through the art colonies of La Jolla and Malibu, and driving north to the galleries of San Francisco.

He bought his first home in Los Angeles, unpacked his trunks, and hung his paintings. He soon amassed a collection of fine art books and literature, including the works of Sir Arthur Conan Doyle, whose Sherlock Holmes was a favorite. Triana may have empathized with the detective as he painstakingly deciphered every phrase, for he, too, solved mysteries of motion and emotion. Antonio was never at a loss for students and it was a time for sunshine and relaxation. His studio prospered, and he was content.

Then Carmen Amaya unexpectedly arrived to film a dance sequence which never appeared. Her work was so extemporaneous that she never remembered her steps in any particular order. To the horror of the MGM technicians, Carmen's movements did not synchronize with the dance she had previously recorded. She was replaced in *Panama Hattie* by the tap-dancing Nicholas Brothers.

Sol Hurok was determined to bring together again his two "turbulent forces of nature." He contacted Triana in his studio. They met in Hurok's Beverly Hills hotel suite, and after hours of haggling, followed by bracing rounds of vodka, plans were put in action for two Hollywood Bowl performances. For these, Triana was to complete his choreography for Ravel's *Bolero*, mount a new version of the entire *El Amor Brujo*, and stage a "Café Flamenco" scene to close the program.

Thus began an arduous training period for many of his students. Some chosen for the production had never appeared onstage before. They sorely needed experience to make them professionals, but their fears were overcome by the zealous spirit pervading the studio, and the sobering sense of responsibility suddenly thrust upon them.

Maurice Ravel, a composer of the French school, created *Bolero* for the Russian dancer Ida Rubinstein. The work was first produced as a Diaghilev ballet in 1928. Ravel's mother was Basque, and so the life of much of his music was turned to Iberia. His *Alborada del Gracioso* was written in homage to long-forgotten Spanish "Morning Songs." His *Bolero* is a musical tour de force. One pictures Don Quixote's windmills rotating endlessly in the breezes of La Mancha. The insistent rhythm never varies.

To Triana, the monotonous drums simulated the pulse of the Spanish soil. As the single theme in the key of C Major repeats and repeats, rising in gradual crescendo,

Antonio Triana and Carmen Amaya in the rehearsal studio

Antonio's choreographic intent was to trace in movement the development of the Spanish style, from the stately classic "Bolero" school to the languorous Andalucian patterns. He and Carmen would dance in counterpoint to the ensemble.

Hollywood lacked male Spanish dancers, so the casting of the Spectre in the *Amor Brujo* posed a problem. Triana preferred not to use a ballet dancer, for however technically effective one might be, he would possibly be emotionally inadequate. The role of the sly, cynical ghost requires the gypsy's spirit of cunning and vengeance. In the "Danza del Terror," during which Candelas is pursued by the apparition, Falla incorporated the tempo of the typical Tanguillo of Cádiz, and it is only successful when the movements and feeling are as natural to the central character as walking itself.

Finally, Antonio turned to the guitarist, Paco Amaya. Surely, he reasoned, if the young gypsy had the dance in his fingers he would have it in his feet as well. In rehearsal, Triana was glad to see that he had not been wrong. Paco would be a sleek, grinning phantom. And rather than use just one dancer in the "Fuego Fatuo" scene, where the girl Lucía flirts with the Spectre and distracts him, the choreographer used three. This was to withstand the disadvantage of the Hollywood Bowl's vast stage, where a single dancer could become lost.

Each evening, after the day's teaching was done, rehearsals began and lasted far into the night. Triana's method was definite and organized. The some dozen students chosen to perform were given rapid, concise instructions in stage technique and decorum. Their frantic mothers were presented with the costume sketches Antonio had painstakingly designed, and at every opportunity, he injected them all with confidence.

Nothing was left to chance but the improvisations of the "Café Flamenco" section of the program. Triana rightly took for granted that both he and Carmen would instinctively respond to the sultry rhythms. He staged the Café as the typical Andalucian meeting place, where men and women gather to gossip, to show off, to flirt, to love, and to fight if the occasion arises.

On August 26, 1943, the debut was but hours away when disaster struck. Morris Stoloff, the musical director of Columbia Pictures, was to conduct the Los Angeles Philharmonic Orchestra, and the orchestra was scheduled to play excerpts from Bizet's *Carmen* and Chabrier's *España*, as well as the *Bolero* and *El Amor Brujo*. At the company's orchestra rehearsal a clash of temperaments occurred during the run-through of *Amor Brujo*, for Carmen was uncomfortable on a confined set. Her violent movements had the canvas scenery shaking on its foundations. Her style of dance was only concerned with rhythm, and she paid scant heed to melody. The orchestral score confused her. She danced oblivious to marked entrances, exits and musical cues. Stoloff threw down his baton in despair and refused to conduct for the unpredictable Amaya.

Hurok was now threatened with a cancellation. It was impossible to contract a substitute conductor on such short notice. The Hollywood Bowl was already sold out, and he would suffer a sizable loss in prestige and profit. Distraught, he went to Triana for consolation, and found the answer. Antonio made a hurried call to his brother, who had arrived in Los Angeles to attend the momentous event.

"Get your tuxedo out of mothballs and be here in twenty minutes!" Antonio yelled over the wires.

As Secretary of Falla's Orquesta de Cámara and its first oboeist, Manolo was more than familiar with *El Amor Brujo*. He had committed most of Falla's compositions to memory. It was not even necessary for him to consult the "partitura" or score. After one rehearsal, he conducted opening night with authority and conviction. A standing ovation ended the concert. The *Bolero* and Triana's splendid "Zapateado" earned rave reviews.

The two performances were hailed as remarkable achievements in dance, by public and press alike. Few were aware that for most of the show, Triana stood in the wings, mimicking the pantomime to the Amayas, pushing them on and pulling them off the stage, as the drama required. The role of puppeteer was not one he relished, and when Hurok asked him to repeat the success at the Metropolitan Opera House, he declined. He would have had to repeat the experience of training all new dancers, this time on the East Coast. His nerves would never stand such an encore. . . .

And although Hurok was grateful for the last-minute reprieve, to the surprise of all

Antonio Triana and Carmen Amaya – "Café Flamenco"

concerned, his gratitude did not exceed the one hundred dollars he paid the wizard conductor!

Even so, Sol Hurok was a reputable showman, whose own work was not easy. He had to worry about publicity, and all the expenses fell on his shoulders. These included salaries, transportation, production and technical work, printing, and innumerable long-distance calls. He had to recruit a stage manager for lighting and curtain cues, and preferably one who could speak seven languages. Box office receipts had to allow for all this, with something left over for his own profits. The risks were many. If performers did not draw an audience, an entire season would prove a total loss. If one became ill, the impresario lost all his advance ticket sales and deposits.

On the other hand, a greedy manager can take advantage of his artists, who rarely have shrewd business minds, and squeeze seven or more concerts, plus matinees, into one week. Artists are anxious to perform, to show ability, to master a theatrical situation. If an impresario suffers through a bad season, it can be balanced by a successful one, but a performer's career can be ruined forever by a short period of unwise direction. He will bail his impresario out of a crisis or emergency, but five minutes after the show, it is too late to make demands. Triana knew this well.

He next set about establishing a stronghold for Spanish dance in California. The Hollywood area became a haven for followers of various kinds. Antonio's pupils were budding ethnographers, who insisted that Spanish dance alone blended European, African and Oriental cultures into one; painters and sculptors, who saw his dance as artistically relevant to their own work; ballet dancers, who appreciated his definite and solid technique, which rejected the uniformity of the classical ballet; modern dancers who were tired of clenched fists and sought self-expression and emotional lift; and professionals, whose dance careers would be their lives.

Triana developed a teaching process which satisfied them all. For basic heelwork technique, he introduced his "zapateado" step, which in action involves the toe and heel of one foot immediately followed by the heel and flat of the other. His beginning classes stressed coordination and technique, and as the pupils matured in knowledge and muscle power, he provided the inspiration which makes the difference between artistry and mechanics.

He also proceeded to explode the myth that unless a child began to dance at the age of seven or eight, there was little possibility of ever achieving technical excellence. Triana discovered that if one is given carefully scheduled lessons at any age, there is no reason why one should not be able to attain a full command of Spanish dance in four or five years, at least from the technical standpoint. The dancer's artistry must always depend upon inherent talent and opportunity for constructive stage experience.

Antonio's students marveled at his stamina. He could teach for hours without rest, leaving breathless, exhausted pupils in his wake. "Tired already?" he reproached, "I'm just getting warmed up!" He nurtured a generation of dancers who clicked their heels up and down the aisles of supermarkets and unconsciously hammered their heelwork in front of Hollywood newsstands, while poring over the latest edition of *Dance Magazine.*

California and the Southwest portion of the United States have the rhythms of Spain as part of their culture. Adobe houses crowned with red curved Mediterranean tiles, patios and orange groves all borrow from Spanish tradition. The Conquistadores who walked there saw the world through the colored glass of their own courage and purpose. They left their vitality as inheritance to succeeding generations of Spanish-speaking people.

The fiestas and mission plays of San Gabriel and Santa Barbara gave the Mexican community of Los Angeles its first opportunity to give full expression to pride of heritage through dance when Triana began to arrange and stage productions for those occasions. In recreating the legends and romantic lore of the "vaqueros" and ranchos along the Camino Real, he gave a colorful glimpse of the history and spirit of an indigenous civilization.

With the now well-trained and highly competent dancers of his studio, Triana started to build his professional company. He knew that a smooth transition to the stage could only be accomplished by constant appearances before increasingly discriminating audiences. The object of class was to learn and improve. In rehearsal, one grew and advanced. Triana criticized and complimented with equal candor. But all guidance is useless if the dancer does not actually experience a living audience across the footlights, and so Antonio provided his pupils with the invaluable experience of performing with him in concerts at the Los Angeles Philharmonic Auditorium, the Wilshire Ebell Theater, the San Francisco Opera House, and the San Diego Bowl.

Composer/Conductor Manuel García Matos (Antonio's brother) with Lola Flores to his right, and her sister Carmen

Jerónimo Villarino, a flamenco guitarist from Huelva, Spain, who had accompanied Triana's New York Museum recitals, was now also living in Los Angeles, and his guitar supplied the creative impulse indispensable for Triana's own flamenco improvisations. This union of talents educated young performers and audiences in the pure tradition of their art. Spanish dance was no longer to be considered a foreign, ethnic invention, but a significant factor on the contemporary theatre scene.

During an average week, Triana taught four or five hours a day, Monday through Saturday. On Sundays, he would put on a pair of tennis shoes and old bathing trunks and run around Griffith Park, "to keep in treem!" He might then drive down the Pacific Coast Highway for an afternoon of bullfights in Tijuana, or stay home and cook paella for guests. To his chagrin, his culinary skill never surpassed that of his friend Señor Wences (the ventriloquist of "It's all right" fame), whose Paella Valenciana was unforgettable.

Never a conformist, Triana was not susceptible to Hollywood social customs or conventions. Instead, he brought Spain to wherever he was, and after a while those around him did as he did.

CHAPTER IX

From time to time, Antonio would receive news of Argentinita. She had appeared with the Ballet Theater, staging and performing *The Three-Cornered Hat* at the Metropolitan Opera House. On the strength of the routines Triana had taught them, she accepted both Manolo Vargas and José Greco to dance with her on what was to be her final concert tour.

In August 1945, Argentinita fell ill again and was rushed to the Harkness Pavilion of the Medical Center in New York. She underwent two operations, but on September 25, after a long coma, one of the greatest performers of her day died. For Triana, it was the end of an era, an irrevocable loss, and for him, no one in the dance world would ever be able to take her place.

Manolo Vargas, José Greco and Pilar sadly accompanied her on her last journey home to Spain, where Pilar was to form her own Ballet Español, continuing Argentinita's choreography and classicism. In his years with Pilar, Manolo gained considerably in technique and began to dance with greater control and command than ever before. His savage good looks and flashing smile gave to his flamenco interpretations a dashing "gitano" character. José Greco, in time, surrounded himself with some of Spain's brightest talents and traveled abroad.

On both sides of the Atlantic, Pilar López and Triana continued to be faithful custodians of the true Spanish dance. They experimented in choreography with sincerity and humility, never straying from tradition and truth. This is not to say that there can be no progress, but that if modernization brings destruction, it defeats its own purpose.

An example was the dancer, Vicente Escudero, who tried to modify Spanish dance years ago. His dance became more eccentric than artistic. Impressed by Picasso and the trend of cubism in his Paris days, Escudero would appear wearing one blue dancing boot and one white one. He tried to create an abstract flamenco, moving in spite of the rhythm, rather than in combination with it. The inner chaos of the artist can never be more appealing than the beauty or even the homeliness of reality. When one can improve on the past, change is justifiable, but when it leads to aberration and is called modern, it is mere distortion which cannot endure.

In July of 1946, Triana appeared at the Hollywood Bowl again, in a new production of the opera *Carmen*, for which he choreographed the gypsy tavern scene of Act II. The principal performers included Winifred Heidt, as Carmen, the Metropolitan Opera House tenor, Ramón Vinay, as Don José, and Marina Koshetz, as Micaela.

An imaginative piece of staging called for the smugglers' chorus of Act III to make a breathtaking descent down the Hollywood mountains on horses and burros. The natural outdoor setting, with its bright stars and craggy cliffs, served as a perfect background for the well-loved Bizet opera.

In Act II, Bizet has his heroine dancing, playing castanets and singing one of her most difficult arias. It is a super-human task, impossible for most sopranos, and so Triana thoughtfully sat his Carmen on a central table and let her seductive voice provide the incentive for the revelry, and for Triana's inspired dancing which followed.

Early in production, Antonio met with Leopold Stokowski, and together they discussed and agreed on the tempo for the dance. In final rehearsal, however, the Maestro was carried away by the ensuing tragedy and conducted the spirited entrance into Lillas Pastia's inn as if it were a march of doom. Triana stopped in his dancing tracks and, in view of the trembling producer, Boris Morros, approached the podium.

"No one interrupts me in rehearsal!" warned Stokowski.

"The tempo is allegro," insisted Triana. "This is a fandango, not a funeral!"

"I'm going back to Philly!" bellowed Stokowski, who had just concluded a long reign as conductor with the Philadelphia Symphony Orchestra.

Yet the iron-willed Stokowski, who was thought incapable of compromise, now did compromise on matters of pace and phrasing. He was impressed, or possibly amused by Triana's audacity, and after an exemplary performance, was the first to compliment Antonio.

As part of the overture to Act IV, Triana danced the rarely performed "Pastorale," from the *L'Arlesienne Suite, No. 2.* Frequent sojourns in the Pyrenees had left an indelible mark on Bizet's compositions, and Triana found this broadly flowing melody adapted easily to Spanish mood and sentiment.

He returned to the Hollywood Bowl that same year in concert, to dance the Sarasate "Zapateado," accompanied by solo violin. Whispering strings joined the purring tremolo of Antonio's heelwork, and together, two impeccable musicians broke the stillness of the summer evening with their serenade of Spanish cadenzas.

Eventually, Triana was involved with film work, although he never found it satisfactory. Dance as art in Hollywood motion pictures had not advanced rapidly enough in his time. Progress has been made more recently, as in the Jerome Robbins, Michael Kidd, and Bob Fosse films, where the dances appear faithful to the choreographer's original intention, and have remained intact.

The main attraction of film for dancer or choreographer is earning a livelihood. The field of dance as entertainment is bound to be more profitable than that of dance as art. In motion pictures, scaled for an audience of millions, only a few basic themes can successfully be employed. Dancing on screen must appeal to a mass audience and cater to modern taste, whatever that may be. Variations are limited and in Spanish dance sequences, the attempt was always to "do the same old thing."

In a film, Spanish dance may support the plot, but must never obscure it. It may decorate and assist dramatic action, but never at the expense of dialogue. The dance must never predominate or distract the audience from the story, and the idiosyncrasies of producer or director must also be respected. What is more, he does not look favorably on a choreographer who wishes to experiment for an unusual effect. Last-minute changes are always called for, and when the problem arises of cutting fifteen or twenty seconds out of a scene, it is the dance which inevitably feels the snip of the scissors. The last word always rests with an executive or the editor.

In the twenty or more films in which Triana choreographed or appeared himself, he was always hampered artistically, for his dance was the art form, with no slick entertainment formulae. He relied upon research, study and technical discipline, rather than gimmicks or flashy appeal. And, although he knew the grief of seeing some of his best efforts on the cutting room floor, some fine moments remain. These include a "Farruca" he arranged for a Gregory Ratoff production, in which the erratic David Lichine performed in Spanish-Cossack style, to Triana's dubbed-in heelwork. There are also the "Polo" danced at the Viceroy's court, in *The Bridge of San Luis Rey*; Richard Allen's aristocratic "Farruca," performed for Ava Gardner in *Snows of Kilimanjaro*; the "Zapateado" for Sarita Montiel in Mario Lanza's last film, *Serenade*; and Carroll Baker's "Flamenco" in the Warner Brothers production of *The Miracle*.

Not every star can dance well after a few lessons, but Triana was able to teach them all the necessary fundamental movements and exercises. The finished dances were beautiful in their simplicity, and also fit into the dramatic situation. All actors are extremely observant, but Carroll Baker was a particularly adept pupil. Perhaps her Method training enabled her for a time to "be" the gypsy dancer she was portraying.

Triana himself was the one individual who tried to raise the Spanish "routine" in films to a high level, so as to justify artistic consideration. Fortunately, he possessed a strong constitution, and realized that dance on film is not sacred, but just a plastic substance, subject to remolding at all times. At least he had the satisfaction of knowing that he demanded typical, rather than pseudo-Spanish costumes and settings for the dances he conceived, and the dances themselves were honest and authentic.

Meanwhile, in New York, in 1957, the pianist José Iturbi had turned his attention to the baton, and was to conduct *El Amor Brujo* and *La Vida Breve* for four performances at the New York City Center Theatre. To the purist, the role of the gypsy girl of Granada who falls dead at the feet of her unfaithful lover in *La Vida Breve* (The Short Life) surpasses that of Carmen in representing the nature of the Andalucian woman. The soprano, Consuelo Rubio, was brought from Madrid to sing Salud, and Muntanola's scenery was borrowed from Barcelona's Liceo Theatre.

The house was sold out way in advance of opening night, but during the last two weeks of rehearsal Iturbi became more and more troubled by the New York dancers' interpretation of the ballet. He confided his doubts to the director, Jean Dalrymple, who agreed that an S.O.S. to Triana would be in order. It was late in the day, and Triana flew to New York with small hopes of saving the foundering show. He felt like a new captain placed on the bridge of a sinking ship, but, as a matter of conscience, he would try to interject at least some measure of artistic merit into the New York premiere of Falla's great masterworks.

In less than two weeks, he re-staged and re-choreographed the entire *El Amor Brujo*, and himself danced Carmelo. In a last-minute switch, and at Iturbi's insistence, a pupil from Triana's Hollywood studio, Rita Vega, who had come along to assist in rehearsals, took on the lead role of Candelas.

El Amor Brujo was commendable, but Triana was not gratified. Better results would have been obtained if he had had the opportunity of casting the dancers himself. He was in the unfortunate and frustrating position of having to simplify his technique to meet limited abilities. Furthermore, the dancers originally scheduled to perform in *El Amor Brujo* were allowed to fulfill their contracts by appearing in *La Vida Breve*, and their indifferent performance did not aid the overall production.

During Antonio's absence from New York, many startling changes had taken place, and he was disturbed by the Spanish Dance activities. There seemed to be a plague of ambition and a dearth of talent. Rehearsal studios erupted with deafening stamps and bangs, having little in common with Spanish art or rhythm. Local concerts dealt mainly in superficialities adorned in sequins and lace. Without contrast of image or mood, the choreography was predictable. The women's skirts were too short and the routines with their effeminate partners, unhappily too long.

Equally distressing were the "Flamenco Lectures and Demonstrations," lengthy discourses which dissected Spanish dance with the scientific coldness of an autopsy. To Triana's way of thinking, it was abhorrent to try to set down rules or contrive meanings or explanations of the flamenco dance, since by its very rebellious unrestrained nature, it challenges definition.

The following commentary which Antonio wrote at the time clearly illustrates his reflections on the matter:

> **"In order to dance Flamenco, one must be Andaluz and have lived and known the first period of the twentieth century. One would have had to attend the "college" of the Andaluz; that is, the fairs, the fiestas, the celebration of the Cruz de Mayo, the bullfights. . . . In the early morning hours on the way to school, one would have had to observe the rich "señoritos" returning from their nocturnal merry-making, taking leave of their friends and still smelling from the Manzanilla (sherry), the mysterious aroma of the flamenco orgy. . . . The dancers shake the layers of dust from their ruffles and still huddle in a group with the singers and guitarists thinking of their "tips." The young gentlemen begin giving money to one and then to another, and finally gesture to their friends, "You take care of that one, I'm going home to sleep."**
>
> **The blazing sun of eight am. illuminates the pale, opaque faces of the revelers, and the group of "flamencos," thinner now, begins to disperse in different directions, murmuring protests as to the small amounts of money they were given. They direct themselves through the small streets and narrow alleys, bestowing mutual invitations in their hoarse voices, "Come to my house, we'll have coffee. . . ." "Sorry, no. My father isn't feeling well. . . ."**

Flamenco is born of sentiment, observation, and reverie. All are ingredients which defy analysis and can hardly be taught. American dancers should never be denied the freedom to study, learn, or interpret the Spanish dance if they are artistically motivated towards it. Many times, it is the foreigner rather than the native Spaniard who, through unwavering desire and persistence, becomes expert in the dance. The question remains, however, whether they should have the right to teach it if, when they do, they breed a generation of imitators. The problem is that out of professional self-preservation and a deficiency in true creativity, many teach only a simplified version of their own techniques and routines. Their pupils, in turn, do the same, until at last there is more emphasis on method than artistry.

In classical ballet, a proficient technician may perform pleasant formations and get by with a high degree of discipline alone. Choreography is carefully preserved, and there is never the need to improvise. If the Spanish dancer cannot create, however, he stagnates. He will depend on the efforts and ideas of others, and, what is worse, he will copy.

Triana left for Europe confident in his belief that such violations of style and alien trends must eventually disappear.

Antonio Triana teaching Sarita Montiel for the Warner Bros. film "Serenade"

Antonio's original words are as follows:

"Para bailar bien Flamenco, hay que ser Andaluz y haber vivido o conocido el primer periodo del siglo 20; haber ido al colegio Andaluz, haber frecuentado las veladas, las ferias, las cruces de Mayo, las corridas de toros . . . haber contemplado por las mañanas, camino del colegio, a los señoritos ricos de regreso de sus juergas nocturnas en las plazas, despidiéndose de sus amigos oliendo a Manzanilla, con ese aroma misterioso de la orgia flamenca . . . apeándose de los coches a las bailaoras, cantaores y los chistosos arrimados, buzcando algo de propina . . . los señoritos ricos dando dinero a unos y otros y repitiendo a sus amigos, "Encárgate tú de eso, que yo me voy a dormir."

Y el sol maravilloso de las ocho de la mañana, iluminando las caras opacas y pálidas de los juerguistas. . . . Los flamencos en grupos poco menos que corriendo en diferentes direcciones, protestando siempre del poco dinero que les habían dado, dirigiéndose por los callejones y invitándose mutuamente, "Vénte a mi casa y tomamos café. . . ." "No, que mi pare no se siente bien. . . ."

CHAPTER X

Immensely proud of his American citizenship, Triana yet remained a citizen of the world. Because of his dance, which set no boundaries, he was free to travel the globe. Although he acknowledged the scientific advancements of his century, he was basically a product of an older creation. And so, he went to Rome and for the first time tiptoed through the hushed cathedral of St. Peter, to gaze in awe at the *Pietá*, and then on to the Sistine Chapel, where he returned day after day to contemplate Michelangelo's magnificent ceiling. Antonio walked through the ancient basilicas, absorbing the wonders of the past, and inhaling its incensed air. He investigated the patterns of small Mediterranean villages, planned in the Middle Ages so as to escape the burning rays of the sun. He traveled to Naples and Pompeii, where he jammed his pockets full of petrified lava and rock, in hope of capturing some tiny particle of a lost civilization.

He bought several paintings and antiques to add to his collection, and once back in America, decided to do some painting himself. Antonio had always been able to draw, with scrupulous attention to detail. He had long ago invested in an easel. Now, with charcoal in hand, he began sketching a kaleidoscope of memories . . . a bridge in Paris, a Venetian canal, a bullfight, the madonna-like faces of the Andalucian women. . . . And Triana painted as Triana danced, with perfection of structure and anatomy, with the exactness of classicism: but never forsaking a dream or vision.

He knew many artists, but cherished most the friendships he formed with Nicolai Fechin, Will Foster, and Carlos Ruano Llopis. The Russian-born Fechin is now valued highly as a portrait artist. His work belongs more to America than Russia, for he painted the Apache, Pueblo and Navajo Indians of the Southwest with a penetrating understanding of the Indian character which is unequalled. He saw Triana dance on many occasions, and often painted him, revealing the hidden nature of the "Andaluz," which he expressed in rampant color in the tilt of Triana's nose and the flicker of an eyelid. Fechin was particularly moved by the Peruvian "Huayno," which Triana had choreographed anew for his company. Perhaps the artist found the equal of his beloved Tartar past in the mood of the Inca.

Antonio remembered him nimbly running up and down the spiral staircase of his home in Santa Monica with cups of dark Russian tea. Then, settling into thoughtful conversation, Fechin would absent-mindedly carve odd bits of wood into sculptured figures which are in treasured collections today.

The National Academician, Will Foster, founded no school, expounded no new theories. His still lifes were masterful, but portraiture was his consuming avocation and the keynote of his art. His portrait of Triana, so realistic and true to life, suggests the style of John Singer Sargent. Foster was an independent thinker whose works were tender and compassionate, whether the subjects were voluptuous nudes or Maine lobsters.

Carlos Ruano Llopis was born in Alicante, Spain. An intense "aficionado" of the bullfight, he devoted his life to painting its surging color and drama. When Twentieth Century Fox filmed *Blood and Sand*, Llopis was the one artist who could render the theme on canvas. He created significant paintings for pictorial advertising, and many of his bullfight posters now hang proudly in museums. He caught the danger of the bullring and the heartbeat of the flamenco with the same masterly brush, for few artists have sensed so well the Spanish character, at work or play.

In his later years, Llopis maintained his studio in Mexico City, where Triana was a

Rita and Antonio Triana together in "Por Soleares"

frequent guest. The artist's painting of *Triana and Pilar*, in a pose from their "Farruca" is an outstanding example of his skill. Joselito, Belmonte, Gaona, Triana—Carlos Ruano Llopis painted them all.

There exists an obvious analogy between the Spaniard and the American, in that neither can claim purity of blood line. Both are products of racial mixtures clinging to their own heritages and traditions, for the Spaniard has Moorish, Roman, Celtic and Jewish blood, and the American his own distinctive set of transplanted genes. These mixtures have enabled the composers of both countries to create music which is romantic, realistic, impressionistic, patriotic, sensuous and sentimental.

Triana believed that the greatest American music is Jazz and the Blues, for, like the Flamenco, they speak to the heart. Pure Jazz and Blues stand alone as a primitive form of self-expression: talented, sincere, and vital. Like Flamenco, Jazz has never lost its spontaneity. It may or may not influence other music, but in its true form it is never superficial entertainment. It raises spiritual and intellectual powers, but cannot be cultivated, for it grows as a wild flower.

Among Antonio's happiest memories was the time he spent with the great black American tap-dancer John Bubbles, of Buck and Bubbles, in the smoking car of a Pullman train. There the two compared and traded foot rhythms and wailed their sorrowful combination of Blues and Flamenco, as the speeding train carried them into the night.

Triana did not base his dance on an existing national form. He created his own, and stamped it with the soul of his people. His dance was Spanish, but it was of himself, too, for often his creations came out of local color. This was the case with Rikitrún, who roamed the streets of Seville when Triana was still a boy. He was a both comic and tragic figure, typically Sevillano, who used his natural wit, rhythm and dance instinctively whenever the opportunity arose to earn a peseta or two. Rikitrún was the personification of the eternal Andalucian theme; the struggle of man against regimentation. From him Antonio devised the character he called "Bailarín de la Calle," or "The Street Dancer."

Bits of a melody from a "Tanguillo" Triana had heard years before in the Puerto Maria section of Cádiz became the prevailing strain in the score Antonio himself composed for his dance, which he decided to premiere at the Palace of Fine Arts in Mexico City. The curtain rose on a darkened stage, and a spotlight sought out and revealed Triana leaning on a somewhat tired lamp post he had salvaged from the theatre's collection of discarded props.

As Triana danced, he pondered if he could indeed bring Rikitrún to life again. The explosion of applause when he finished gave him the answer. In a twinkling, he had become the Andalucian character who danced on the street for money. Magically, he made everyone feel the inimitable rhythm in his burst of spirit, followed by an impudent succession of movements. But then the ego was trapped once more by the rules of social order and restriction. The character moved on. With a Chaplinesque shrug, he turned a corner and went elsewhere, always in search of his own personal miracle.

The content of Triana's dance was so human that his genius became accepted as universal. He knew that dance and music can never be separated, even though each is beauty in itself. The choreographer's feeling for the music must inevitably determine whether his creation will be appropriate to it. The dance is always ephemeral. Because of the constant motion, one impression is immediately erased by the next.

Primitive dance stresses repetition, equal balance of steps, and musical phrases. Somehow, familiar monotonous motion is consoling to the spirit. Theatre dance, however, must introduce the element of contrast which goes together with the proportion and harmony. This was never forgotten in Triana's choreography.

His next major work was the "Gypsy Song" which ends the *Capriccio Espagnol*, by Nicholas Rimsky-Korsakov. This fantasy for violin and orchestra was composed when Rimsky-Korsakov was still a naval cadet. The Spanish music he heard during his short stay in Cádiz made him aware of the possibility for vast orchestral effects. The entire *Capriccio* shows the composer's gift in handling orchestral arrangements. He was able to absorb the Spanish ambiance, the contrast between the biting cold gray Russian winters and the sun-baked skies of Andalucia. He was sensitive to gruff Russian voices giving way to soft Spanish falsettos. This brilliant score inspired Triana to a dance distinguished by dazzling theatrical form.

Antonio carried on a ceaseless search for perfection. He tried new choreographic arrangements for the "Suite Iberia," the danzas of *La Vida Breve*, Turina's "Orgia," and his own flamenco creations of the "Alegrías," "Caña," "Zapateado," or "Farruca." He sought fresh entrances and anything else which promised to add to his art. Change was not overnight, but a sure continuing process, the product of intelligent thought and experimentation.

Today, in countries where dance is not subsidized, it is difficult, if not impossible, to keep a supporting group together for sufficient rehearsal time, since remuneration is usually based on one or two concerts. Few Spanish dance companies can afford scenic designers or extravagant musical accompaniment. The elite have always patronized classical ballet, possibly to be seen, rather than to see.

When Spanish dance devotees witness a first-class performance, they are given a standard by which to base their judgment. These were the people Triana hoped to interest and convince, for he knew that the Spanish dance is an art worthy of enthusiastic support. An idealist, he had the austere pride of the Spanish Dancer, and was unwilling ever to be less than that. The tremendous drive of his work was not there by chance. He depended a great deal on improvisation, but his attitude was never bohemian, and that improvisation was whipped into shape by years of dedication. It was his coherent mind, together with rare intuition, which marked his dance as truly superior.

In pursuing his goals, Triana never escaped his share of human failings, mistakes, misunderstandings, shattered illusions or broken dreams. As every man also has triumphs, joys, sorrows and disasters, he knew his moments of ecstasy and countless disappointments. He was obsessive, impulsive, keenly observant, sensitive, and ardent. The elements of excitement and success in his life, together with his enormous charm, endeared him to women, and he, in turn, was always attracted to them. But he did take time and care to love and marry one in particular. His son, Antonio II, was born in 1958, followed by his daughter, Felipa, in 1960.

All his life, Antonio had a mania for collecting things: letters, drawings, old address books of friends in various countries, hundreds of photographs and news clippings. Had he not traveled so much and mislaid trunks en route, he would have been encumbered with far more belongings than he knew what to do with.

As the years went by, he followed his destiny as a teacher of Spanish dance, and did his best to ignore the changing world. It was always easier for him to dance than to make conversation. Yet, despite all the time he spent living away from Spain, he never lost the unexpected wit or unmistakable accent of the "Andaluz." He found great pleasure in a small glass of manzanilla, in paper-thin slices of "jamon serrano," a new painting, and the laughter and movement of people around him. A boyish-looking man at thirty and forty, Triana maintained his boundless energy and good looks into his sixties and seventies. Master of his craft, he taught until he was 78!

Of the dance, he would say, "Ay, Carmen is gone too. It is an age of mediocrity!" To his children: "Practice ... todos los días ... aivrewhaire ... aivrewhaire...."

Wherever Triana was, wherever he taught, wherever he danced became a focal point for artistic creative expression. He devoted much of his time to teaching his children his dance, and of all his possessions, it is the most priceless legacy they could ever hope to inherit. I am at all times aware of how fortunate they are, for I am their mother.

But that, as they say, is another story.

America grows and evolves. Changes take place more rapidly and perhaps more basically than elsewhere. Human, material, and spiritual resources are in such abundance and of such quality that an improved way of life for the people is, in one sense, inevitable. But if life is to be as sound, rewarding, and sustaining as possible, it is essential that we do not lose that sense of continuity with the past, that strong awareness of all that has gone, in terms of human effort and imagination into the making of this New World.

It was no accident that El Paso, Texas, was chosen by Antonio Triana for his retirement home, surrounded as it is by the very essence of its Spanish forebears. As a dancer, teacher, and choreographer, he loved this land deeply and enduringly. As artist, he gave shape, meaning, and immortality to the raw material of its heritage. The aura of the Old World still lingers over El Paso. The influence of Spanish and Indian cultures is still seen in the bilingual community. One feels the spirit of the copper-hued Indian, the genial Mexican, the dauntless Spanish soldier, and the enterprising "Americano." The sands of the Chamizal have witnessed the coming and going of generations.

The Spaniards came up from Mexico with zeal. Eagles soared overhead, rabbits scurried underfoot as the dusty paths were beaten into the face of the earth. They left mathematics, Holy Scriptures, astronomy, and music on their way. They left footprints, and they left their soul prints.

At his outstanding school of Ballet Español in El Paso, Triana's traditional Spanish dance and the folklore of the Southwest flowed together in a single stream, bringing inexhaustible richness to the art. Triana possessed the remarkable power of summing up in a dance the spirit of an entire people. His Spanish dance was a living process, its best traditions constantly developing new traits. Its poetry revealed to his audiences and to his pupils the inestimable treasures ingrained in his own artistic nature.

For the newcomer, bewildered by the complexities of our times, Triana's life was evidence that certain verities are ageless. Inspiration and creation remain a fascinating drama of man's humanity to man.

The children: Antonio II and Felipa

With his memories of another day, Triana gave heartwarming assurance that all had not been forgotten—that much still lived.

Antonio Triana, 1906–1989

Se murió mi mario,
(My husband is dead,)
Se murió mi consuelo.
(My comfort is dead.)
No tengo quien me diga
(I have no one to tell me)
"Ojiyos e terciopelo."
("Your eyes are of velvet.")

PART II

THE SPANISH DANCE

CHAPTER XI

ORIGINS

Three Moorish girls I loved in Jaén,
Axa and Fátima and Marién.

Anon

The dance, the theater, poetry, music, all that we call culture came out of primitive superstition, evolving slowly as the minds and hearts of men sought reason for their being, and found religion. In every civilization, art is founded upon worship.

The cradle of culture was based in two regions: the Nile Basin, and the fertile Crescent of Western Asia, between the Tigris and the Euphrates rivers. History tells of shifting tribes of Semitic, African, and Indo-European races, of the struggle of small states, extending their conquests and building empires, only to be swept away by the tide of succeeding invasions. The major cultures of Egypt, Babylonia, Assyria, and Persia were enriched by contributions from the Hittites and Phoenicians. In Egypt, the environment led to adoration of the Sun and the River Nile. Early Egyptians, preoccupied with thoughts of an afterlife, sang and danced for their gods, Horus, Osiris and Ra.

The ancient Hebrew "Song of Songs" is traditionally ascribed to King Solomon. "Dance for us, princess, dance, as we watch and chant!" begins one of the beautiful verses that communicates the human partnership that sustained creation in Old Testament times. In I Samuel 18, we read that "when David returned from the slaughter of the Philistines ... the women came singing and dancing to meet King Saul." In II Samuel 6, which describes how David carried the Ark of God to Jerusalem, we are told that it was greeted with harps, timbrels or hand drums, and cymbals. Another instrument used by David's procession was the "sistra." The Hebrew name suggests shaking and rattling, and these early castanets of clay were called "sistrum" in Egypt. The Israelites had no musical notation and the men and women danced separately in performance and in ritual.

At one time the African state of Carthage seemed destined to rule the ancient world. The city of Carthage was founded in 800 BC on the coast of what is now known as Tunisia. The Carthaginians arrived in Spain shortly after the Greeks, who brought a culture which produced the greatest drama the world has known. Religious rites in the Greek hill theaters included choric song and dance to honor the gods Apollo and Dionysus. The Peloponnesian War set in motion forces that changed the Greek world. The lands of the Hittites, the Assyrians, the Bablyonians, and the Persians were absorbed into a new Greek empire, so that Hellenic culture became international.

Alexander the Great (356–323 BC) conquered all the old oriental kingdoms, the whole of western Asia, and Egypt in one of the outstanding military feats of all time. An enormous library in his city of Alexandria contained more than 600,000 rolls of papyrus in every ancient language.

Art flourished with the Greeks until Rome defeated both Greece and Asia. In 205 BC, a decisive battle on the banks of the Guadalquivir brought Roman rule to the Iberian Peninsula until about 620 AD. The literary dramatist, Seneca, was born in Córdoba. The poet Martial came from Calatayud, and his Epigrams praise the vineyards of Alicante, the dancers of Cádiz, and their skill with the castanets.

The great Roman amphitheater in Spain was at Tarragona. Here, as elsewhere, one single dancer portrayed all the characters against a musical background of wind and string instruments. It is noted that the soloists wore a sort of clapper under their feet to keep the rhythm. The mighty Roman Empire made Spain the direct heir of ancient civilization, for Rome was the controlling power in the Mediterranean and Latin the foundation of common speech. Under the Emperor Trajan, the empire reached its greatest extent, from Britain to Africa, from Spain to the Caspian Sea.

Eventually, however, the barbarians moved in, during the 4th and 5th centuries AD, when the Germanic Vandals overran Spain and North Africa, together with the Visigoths, who had Teutonic and Saxon ties. Their mountainous strongholds in Spain, including Aragón, Navarra, and Castilla, held until the Arab invasion of 711 AD. One year later, the Arabs brought the art of making paper from Samarkand to Spain, and Spanish art and music were to be profoundly influenced by the newcomers.

Spain, successively stained with Punic, Roman, and Gothic blood, now absorbed in just a few generations the dialects and manners of the Semites of the Arabian peninsula and the Moors of Morocco. And the Arabs allowed their Moslem brethren to share in the conquest. Egyptians entered their settlements at Murcia and Lisbon. The royal legion of Damascus was planted at Córdoba. The natives of Yemen and Persia were scattered throughout Toledo. The fertile lands of Granada were bestowed to ten thousand horsemen of Syria and Iraq. To the Berbers from the Algerian hills, the Arabs grudgingly assigned the bleak central Spanish plateau, reserving for themselves the rich valleys to the south. This was a time when the Arabian caliphs granted Jews and Christians religious liberty for the payment of a small tribute.

By 930 AD, Córdoba, Spain, was the center of Arab learning, science, and art. Arabs ruled all that is Andalucia from the eighth to the fifteenth century, so Arabic influence in Spain's music and dance is an important factor. There was no particular national dance, for all the Arabic arts were the product of scattered dissimilar peoples, united only by their common faith in Islam.

El Cid began the overthrow of Moslem rule by fighting across the Spanish plains until his death in 1099, and Christianity gained control with the Battle of Navas de Tolosa in 1212. This led from the Middle Ages to the glorious Renaissance of new intellectual curiosity across Europe. As the court of Ferdinand and Isabella gave credibility to scientific discovery – including that of Christopher Columbus in 1492 – Granada was taken from the Moors, and they were finally vanquished in Spain. This did not, however, lead to freedom for the art of dance. During the terrible years of the Spanish Inquisition little was heard of music and dancing, although they could not be stamped out. One sufferer from the Inquisition was the great Miguel de Cervantes. Born in 1547, he preferred folk music to so-called art music, as did his contemporary, Shakespeare. Companies of dancers are mentioned in the philosophical novel *Don Quixote*, which describes men with swords and bells, shaking and leaping like Cornish Morris men, whose dances are said to have originated in Spain. Sole-slappers marked time for them by striking the soles of their feet alternately with their hands.

In the Spain of that period, the Zarabanda was the most wanton of dances. In his work, *Tratado Contra Los Juegos Públicos* (*A Thesis Against Public Displays*), Father Mariano attacked it violently. But it was of little consequence that here and there a priest condemned it, for in the half-century from 1580 to 1630, a dancing mania had seized the Spanish population. "Zarabanda!" was the cry of the dancers gathering in the streets and public squares. The Zarabanda even invaded the churches in its musical form, by using sacred lyrics instead of the objectionable popular refrains. Other popular street dances also infiltrated the church: the "Chacona" and the "Pasacalle."

In 1598, officials of the city of Madrid implored King Phillip II to permit only the good old dances, and ban the new vulgar ones. Finally, in 1630, the Zarabanda was actually prohibited by the Royal Council of Castile because of its erotic movements. By that time, however, it had already been deposed by the Seguidillas and the Chacona, which were even more lascivious.

The Zarabanda had nothing to do with the French Sarabande, which was characteristic of the Suites of the eighteenth century. The Spanish dance is older, and gave the French version its name, but not its rhythm. The Spanish rhythms were later carried to the Americas, and returned transformed as South American Guajiras.

The Chacona was a favorite style of dance in the time of Cervantes. It resembles the modern Chacona of Granada, and has, too, an amazing affinity with the *Violin Sonata in E Major*, by Johann Sebastian Bach. In various aspects it is also reminiscent of Bach's own Chaconnes, and therefore provides an interesting link between Spanish folk art at the beginning of the seventeenth century, and the immortal German, Bach, who was not born until near the end of that century.

Similarly, the Pasacalle is another ancient musical style found later in musical suites of the seventeenth and eighteenth centuries. In three-quarter time, it employs a ground bass, the theme of which occasionally appears in higher parts. It is usually written in a minor key, much like the Chaconne, and Bach brought the music of this dance to its peak of perfection in his *Passacaglia in C Minor*, for the organ.

There was a definite division of the dances of the period into two categories: "bailes" and "danzas," at least in theory, rather than practice. In reality, there was a constant process of blending the two, with aristocratic forms being vulgarized, and folk dances being refined. Eventually, something of each appeared in both. The distinction was due entirely to the manner of performance. "Danzas" were executed lightly and cleverly, but with the feet alone. In the "bailes," however, the whole body would come into action, in a display of gusto and emotion. The difficulties encountered in dancing the "bailes" were in critical contrast with the ease of performing the "danzas." In another connotation, the "danza" was frivolous while the "baile" was considered shameless.

In the words of Cervantes, "No hay mujer española que no salga del vientre de su madre bailadora" – or "There is no Spanish woman who was not born from a dancer's womb."

The Seguidilla, also mentioned in *Don Quixote*, is now familiar to all regions of Spain. In Andalucia there are varieties called Seguidillas Sevillanas and Sevillanas Mollares. In other regions the dance adopts the name of the place: Seguidillas Gallegas, Seguidillas Zamoranas. The origin of all is the Seguidillas Manchegas, and in every interpretation arm positions may vary, but the essence of the original is unaltered.

The Seguidilla Manchega was born on the plains of La Mancha. Named by the Arabs "Al Mancha," or "Dry Land," it is a small territory partly in the kingdom of Aragón and partly in Castile. The Seguidilla is divided into coplas, or verses, and in the old authentic form the music ceases at the end of each and the dancer remains in a frozen position until the opening notes of the next. This immovable stance is called "bien parado," and its element of balance, the use of a stylized pose as finale to a dance, was incorporated into the early Spanish Boleros.

Boleros were the first of their kind to acquire fame in other European countries. The French poet Gautier, after visiting Spain, wrote of their grace and beauty. Bolero derives from the Spanish word volar – to fly – for in many parts of the country there is no distinction in pronunciation between the letters v and b. The Bolero is an animated dance characterized by many steps which today are only used traditionally in the ballet idiom.

In the Baroque period of decorative art, a sense of theatricality gripped the populace, making illusion seem stronger than reality. During the seventeenth century the aristocratic Spanish families who ruled the Italian states cultivated their theatrical taste in Milan and Parma. They carried ideas back to Spain and brought about a revival of the court dances. At that time Phillip IV ruled Spain, and followed his neighboring countries by dancing the Pavanas of the era.

What can be described as "scenic ballets" were also in favor, and sword dances were known from the earliest times. Their vogue was greatest in the kingdom of Toledo. Called "Espata-danzas," these were so popular that in 1660 a hundred men performed one before the king as part of the celebration of Corpus Christi. The dancers, usually farm laborers, wore smocks and linen knee britches, and carried white wooden swords. These were in contrast with the black swords used with rapiers in fencing. Weapons held high, the men executed artistic patterns; in particular, one called "la degollada," in which they tried to "decapitate" their leader, while he gracefully eluded that fate. This dance was performed as late as the end of the nineteenth century in the streets of Madrid at Carnival time, the performers wielding their swords with amazing dexterity.

Polite artists felt contempt for the music of the people, and when they at last condescended to take over the popular pieces they remade them into learned and sacred interpretations. Similarly, instrumental music was separated by class. The nobility danced to small orchestras with harpsichords, lutes, and harps, while the commoners sang and danced to a guitar accompaniment.

A clear glimpse of the folk music of the time may be had in the *Instrucción de Música Sobre la Guitarra Española* (*Instruction of Spanish Guitar Music*), written by Gaspar Sanz and published in Zaragosa in 1674. Music composed by Sanz himself is thoroughly

Spanish, with typically Andalucian cadences. Some phrases were set down according to tradition, whereas others were of his own invention, all written for the contemporary guitar, which had two strings for each note, and a correspondingly fuller tone.

Another seventeenth-century composer was Domenico Scarlatti. Born in Italy in 1685, he spent the latter part of his life as musician and teacher of the royal Spanish court. Like the Spanish monk, Padre Antonio Soler, he composed Spanish dances as sonatas for the harpsichord. They were not known to have played the guitar, as did their contemporary, Padre Basilio, who was famous for his rousing Fandangos. Their compositions for the harpsichord, however, are permeated with the sounds of the village Jotas, Fandangos, and Boleros. They managed to join Spanish popular music with that which was considered suitable for the palaces and cathedrals.

CHAPTER XII

LAND OF THE JOTA

Castile – Vigorous, dry, free land –
Mother of courage and goodness . . . .

Miguel de Unamuno

Dance has always been an instinctive movement in man as he expresses the reactions of his spirit to his surroundings, for nature has gifted him with a sense of rhythm and harmony. In Spain, the people still move in solemn prayer for their newly planted fields, and dance for joy and thanksgiving at the harvest. All forty-nine Spanish provinces have developed styles and movements determined by climate, costumes, and customs.

"Jota" applies both to the song and the dance. There can be no definite opinion as to its origin, but one theory holds that it is named for the Moor, Aben Jot, whose fast, suggestive dances scandalized the Spaniards in the twelfth century. The Jota of Aragón is certainly the lyrical outlet of its region, expressing its very atmosphere. It is manly and courageous in song, and in feeling matches the rough scenery, with its snow-capped peaks, deep valleys and dry plains, swept by strong winds from the Moncayo Mountain, and crossed by the Ebro River. Here live tenacious, strongly-built men and women, guileless, sincere, and outspoken. They possess a healthy optimism and delight in self-expression through lively song and dance. The Jota suits them well.

The dancers are accompanied by their own unique musicians, playing stringed instruments which emphasize the melodies of the loudly chanted coplas. Although styles vary considerably, rhythmical motifs are always much the same, and the "real" Jota is that of Aragón, which has found its way all over the Peninsula. Its verses show a love of place and are often witty and sarcastic. On special occasions, they reverently address the Virgin of the Pilar, or, in Aragonese, Pilarica, but serious or not, they are best summed up by the following verse:

El que no canta la Jota
si ha nacido en Aragón
o es mudo de nacimiento
o no tiene corazón –

which simply states that anyone born in Aragón who does not sing the Jota is either dumb or heartless.

A singer begins with a copla, followed by a musical interlude leading into the exuberant dance. There is the usual balance and rhythm of primitive village choreography; and song and dance alternate throughout. Other regions, such as Alcañiz and Calanda, have a calmer style, and use toes and heels to perform the variations.

The Jota of Zaragosa, however, is light, merry, and challenging in performance. Opinions vary as to the century it stems from, which could be seventeenth, eighteenth, or nineteenth.

An important deviation from the Jota Aragonesa is the Jota Valenciana, with its own particular regional configurations, accompanied by a rustic oboe called the "dulzaina" and a small tamboril, or drum. Songs known as "alboradas" in other parts of Spain are called "albaes" in Valencia. A dance of that area is known as the "Xáquera Vella," and is primarily performed at weddings, although it may appear on other occasions. It is solemn in character, with slow, stately movements, led first by bride and groom, with their sponsors following, and then the entire wedding party. The ceremonious dance ends with couples depositing money in the musicians' hats. There are also other wedding dances, such as Lagartera's "Baile de la Manzana," or "Dance of the Apple." In this, the bride carries an apple cut in two, and whoever wishes to dance with her places coins on the pieces. It is considered in poor taste not to invite her to dance, and not to present money to the happy pair.

In Ibiza, off the coast of Valencia, widows are allowed, after a year in solitude, to dance in public, with dignity and reserve. Other dances on this Spanish isle are known as "La Curta" and "La Llarga," and castanets are the main feature. In Castilla, the Jota Castellana frequently uses castanets attached to the middle fingers and played in a brusque, unemotional manner; unlike that of Andalucia, where they are placed traditionally on the thumbs and given subtle romantic intonations. Much emphasis is placed on the use of castanets in the Canarias and Baleares. These island dances are joyful Jotas, known in the Canarias as "Isa," "Folia," "Serinoque," and "Tajaraste," and as "Copeo" in the Baleares, whereas in Mallorca, the "Mallorquina" is popular.

An important group of Castilian songs has as its basis the "canciones" de Ronda, which are serenades. Singers roam from street to street, leading them to be called "pasacalles," and they are often accompanied, as the dancers are, by a primitive oboe, or "chirimía," and a small drum.

The typical dance of Catalonia is the "'Sardana." The orchestras of ten musicians are called "coblas." A version of the "Sardana," "El Contrapás," appears to be the oldest. It is performed in a circle and custom dictates that couples finish at the exact place on the floor where they began. Another variation, "L'Hereu Riera," is danced on the toes, with intricate steps executed on angles formed by two crossed sticks. The "Ball del Ciri" features six couples, whereas the "Ball de Sant Farriol" is comic in style and performed only by men as grotesques.

Other Jotas are the "Parranda," or "Murciana" of Murcia, the "Extremeña," of Badajoz, and the "Al Pandero," or the "'Brincadillos" of Burgos, in which snapping fingers accompany the flying feet, and women keep their eyes lowered in a demure manner.

Spanish dances do not usually celebrate the rite of passage from childhood to adolescence. However, such a ritual has been performed as a public celebration in Burgos, and is called "Los Santos Inocentes," or "The Holy Innocents." Five or six infants are placed on a mattress in a church courtyard and a dancer with saber in hand gracefully leaps over them. Symbolically, the children have eluded the wrath of King Herod, as did the baby Jesus, and can now grow into adulthood having experienced danger and salvation.

"El Baile Montañés" or "Dance of Mountain Dwellers" begins slowly in a languid fashion and comes to life as the singer begins the first "tercio" or verse. Men and women form lines and the partners cross each other in a braiding design.

Most of the dances of the North are performed in local rope-soled footwear called "alpargatas." They resemble ballet slippers, but without the padded toe. Consequently, there is no heelwork and elevation is important.

Vasconia has purely Basque dances, using no castanets. The steps are complicated and require much agility. Many are performed by men only, and young boys are eager to learn the timeless patterns. The partnered dance called "'Zortzico" or "Aurresku" is presented in a major plaza of the town. It consists of several traditional sections. The first is called "saludo" or greeting, when the men form a circle and the leader throws his beret on the ground. This salute is answered by an authority figure and the lead dancer returns to the formation. "Alzescu" and "Pasamanos" follow, and at one point, the women who are elected to join in assume a dignified pose as their partners toss their berets at their feet and dance around them. The next portion of the dance matches the Aragonese Jota in its vigorous and competitive spirit. "Arin-Arin" ends it all, as the performers introduce steps of their own creations.

Basque dances and other traditions are part of a mysterious past, for the Basque people are not only divided between France and Spain, but possess their own strange language called "Euskara," and claim descent from the lost continent of Atlantis.

To the extreme west of Spain lies Galicia. It is washed by the Atlantic, and its coast is rugged and beautiful, as are its mountains, where heights and valleys are wrapped in mists rising from the abundant rains. The people of Galicia are by nature thoughtful and serene.

The typical musical instrument of this district is the "Gaita," or bagpipes, whose wild and untamed notes are capable of great variation, dominated by one long, drawn-out chord which gives them a melancholy sound. The "Pandeiro" is another musical instrument of the region, which lends its name to a dance. It is square, with lined leather sides and groups of jingles inside. It is ornamented by colored tassels placed on the four corners, and its rhythm, together with a chorus of voices, provides accompaniment for a tempestuous dance.

Most typical of Galicia, though, is the "Muñeira," which has two forms: "Ruada" and "Fuliada." Before the Greek invasion, tribes living in Galicia had their own dance, and proof exists that among the Celtic peoples there were ritual dances performed at full moon. These resembled some which still exist in other Celtic countries: Scotland, Wales, Cornwall and Ireland; but the rhythms of today's versions differ greatly from the "Muñeira." It must be assumed that the only absolutely Celtic detail which remains in Spain is the "Gaita," and although the "Muñeira" is wholly Spanish, it does contain the last remnants of Celtic tradition in the country. In one version, it is danced in single couples. This is called "Ribeirana," and it is faster, with more figures than the usual "Muñeira." Its name comes from its district of origin. Because these are peasant people, their enthusiasm for dance is dependent upon good crops and clement weather.

In discussing provincial dance, mention must be made of the "Albadas," "Auroras," "Bodegas," "Gozos," "Mandamientos," "'Mayors," "Oliveras," "Pasiones," "Salves," and "Villancicos de Navidad," which are Christmas and New Year songs and dances.

CHAPTER XIII

THE NEW WORLD

*We sailed up the coast to where the
sun set and we reached a great river.*

Bernal Diáz del Castillo

Almost a hundred years before the settlement of the first permanent colony in New England, the Spaniards had established schools in Mexico for the teaching of their music. The first of these was founded by Pedro de Gante at Texcoco, in 1524, only three years after Cortés had captured the city. The early missionaries left several accounts of the musicality of the native Indians, who used music and dance in all their religious and civic ceremonies, as well as in their public and private festivities. Because so much of it was associated with their religion, and therefore regarded as heathenish, the Spaniards destroyed Indian music, rather than preserved it. As early as 1583, Christian hymns and psalms were translated into the Mexican language as an important step in weaning the natives from their pagan faith.

The two great centers of Spanish culture in early colonial times were Mexico City in the north and Lima, the Peruvian capital, in the south. Spanish drama was almost always associated with music and dance, and it flourished in Lima during the sixteenth and seventeenth centuries. The plays of Calderón de la Barca were held in high esteem there, and the popularity of that celebrated Spanish dramatist endured even longer in Peru than in Spain.

The lyric theater played an important part in spreading Spanish music throughout Hispanic America. The more successful Spanish *Zarzuelas* were performed thousands of times, and received with enthusiasm in all the principal cities. At Buenos Aires, for example, Tomás Bretón's *La Verbena de La Paloma* was on one occasion playing in five theatres simultaneously. Since the bulk of music written for the *Zarzuelas* consisted of arrangements of popular airs and dances from various regions of Spain, the effect was to keep alive these traditional rhythms in the New World.

Music also came, sadly enough, with slavery. The Spanish discoverers first tried to enslave the Indians to work the fertile soil of Cuba, Hispaniola and Puerto Rico, which could produce the luxury of sugar for export. Similarly, the Portuguese required slaves to work their coffee plantations in Brazil. It was a missionary, Bartolomé de las Casas, who recommended the importation of African laborers to fill the need.

Slavery was nothing new. This deplorable practice was old when Moses and Christ were young. In Caesar's Rome, men and women, black, brown and white, and their children were sold. For several decades before the beginning of the European trade, Moslem merchants dragged their African prisoners across the sands of the Sahara. In the fifteenth century, Portugal diverted this trade to the Atlantic.

Descendants of these first captives, black Christians born in Spain and Portugal, went with the first European adventurers. Black explorers, servants, slaves, and free men accompanied the Iberians in their expeditions in the New World. They were with Pizarro in Peru, with Cortés in Mexico, and with Menendez in Florida.

Africans cherished their musical heritage. Dance was not art to them: it was life itself. Both their songs and their dances were related to ritual and religion. Bahia, in northern Brazil, seems to have folk music and dance most similar to that of Africa. The polyrhythmic percussion technique and the stressing of syncopation in Africa played a vital role in the development of the Rumba and the Conga as popular dances. The Samba, best-known of Brazilian dances, probably began as a round dance. The accompanying gourds and maracas (seeds or small pebbles in a shaker) bear striking resemblance to the basket rattles of West Africa.

There is no doubt that the Cuban folk melodies and Rumba also echo Spain. The popular music of Andalucia is also to be heard in the Cuban "Guajiras," while the "Zapateado," with its fluent rhythm and heel-strikes, has as its origin the flamenco "Zapateado."

The Tango of Cádiz, mixed with African and Cuban influences, appears to have preceded nearly the whole of South American music. The Tango of Argentina seems to be simply a variant of the "Tango Andaluz," but it has acquired an entirely domestic choreography.

The most widely-known Spanish dances in Chile, Peru, and Argentina were the Bolero, the Fandango, and the Seguidilla. In Chile, the Seguidilla was called "Sirilla," and it is still performed today. It is interesting to note that in the Peruvian dances, "Yaravies," "Cachuas," and "Lauchas," there are traces of Spanish forms, such as the Jota and Sevillanas.

Castanets are rarely used in Mexico or South America, but in many of the folk dances the performers manipulate a "pañuelo," or handkerchief, which plays an expressive role in the choreographic pantomime.

The dances and songs of contemporary Mexico are entirely Spanish in structure. Although the "Jarabe" is thoroughly stamped with the Mexican spirit, it is a descendant of the Spanish "Zapateado," and its rhythm resembles that of the "Mazurka." The Mexican "Huapango" is ultimately traced to the Spanish "Son," while the "Veracruzanas" are totally the "Zapateados," "Tanguillos," and "Tientos" of Cádiz, given a tropical accent. The characteristic dance of Yucatan, the "Jarana," on the other hand, is possibly closer to the melodic and rhythmic foundation of ancient Mexican songs than any other native air in existence today.

A remarkable variant of Spanish musical form is the Mexican "Corrido." It is a development of the Spanish "Romance," in which historical or contemporary events or even trivial gossip may form the subject. Like all Mexican song and dance, it owes a great deal to the characteristic accompanying band, called "Orquesta Típica" in Mexico City, and "Mariachi" in outlying districts.

The "Pasillo" is popular in both Colombia and Venezuela. Tiny Panama has three distinct national dance forms: the "Mejorana," the "Tamborito," and the "Punto." All are Spanish in influence as are the regional dances of Guatemala, called "Son Guatemalteco," and the popular "Pericón" of Uruguay. The typical "Shoe Dance" of the Dominican Republic is known as "Zapateado Montuño," while the topical ballads of almost all Latin American nations resemble the Mexican "Corridos."

In the United States of America, Spanish music has been kept alive by Latin communities in various parts of the country. In Idaho there is a Basque colony where the unique songs and dances of the Basque provinces are still carefully preserved and performed.

In Mexican-American communities, "Los Pastores" are given annually, enacted against the background of a "Nacimiento," or decorated altar, with many figures representing the Nativity scene. The melodies are simple and stirring, and may readily be associated with the traditional Spanish "Villancicos," or Christmas Carols.

Seeking gold in their expeditions, the Spanish Conquistadores were not to know that they brought with them in exchange a more lasting treasure, in their nation's music and dance.

CHAPTER XIV

REGIONAL COSTUMES

Virgin in crinoline, along the river of
the street you ride your ship of lights . . . .

Federico García Lorca

The geographical situation of the Iberian Peninsula is privileged. There is contrast of landscape and of climate and a diversity of races, so Spain possesses a folklore that is one of the richest in the world.

Regional costumes represent all the lines, shades, forms, and colors of ancient apparel in a profusion of infinite mixtures of cultures. There are pendants, ornamental hair combs, earrings, buckles: all sorts of adornments and beads. Some costumes are simple and austere, while others are rich in velvets and brocades. There is beauty overall, and the textures and trimmings move in perfect harmony with the songs and dances. The differences between some Spanish costumes are so distinct that they appear to be of different nations, when in truth they may come from districts separated by only a few kilometers of easy walking distance.

For example, in Alicante, the traditional outfit called "Ibi" is of unusual character. Skirts are of black wool. The waists are sashed with light silk ending in long fringe. The hairstyle is described as classic Levantine; originating by the east shores of the Mediterranean Sea. It is covered by a little hat of black corduroy or velvet, dotted with beadwork.

Typical of Aragón is a black apron worn over a colored skirt. There are white stockings and the sandals called "alpargatas." A large flowered shawl covers the shoulders, its loose ends crossed and tied. The women's hair is worn parted in the middle and drawn into a knot behind the head. There are long, filigree earrings of an almond shape. Costumes are generally the same in both the north and south districts of Aragón, the south perhaps being a bit more fancy and ornate.

The dress of Asturias is much influenced by the regions of Santander and Galicia. Skirts are of red cloth with black trim. Aprons are of the same red cloth, bordered with embroideries and jet beads. A white blouse is worn under a red and black shawl which covers the shoulders. A kerchief in white, knotted around a chignon, completes the outfit.

Badajoz is the wild, remote country of the conquerors. Women in this province wear woolen skirts of white, black, and red stripes. The red waist is covered by a large kerchief of percale, stamped in red and white, called "sandía." The hair is arranged with flowers, as in the neighboring Andalucia.

The people of Catalonia have appropriated their wearing apparel (silks and brocades) from the style of the elegant Spanish court. A white mantilla or veil is called "gandalla." By contrast, hemp sandals are worn with the brocaded, full-waisted skirts.

There are many religious dances in Spain for which particular costumes are worn. The one of Córdoba belongs to the village of Fuente Toja, and consists of a colored skirt and white blouse decked with ribbons. The most notable feature of this outfit is the large hat covered with flowers.

In Extremadura, the dress of "Montehermoso" has two skirts. The first is of a dark red color, the second of a lighter hue. The waist is black and stockings are blue. A large, curious hat is perched on top of a woolen kerchief.

There are three different typical dresses in Galicia and one is similar to the costume of northern Portugal. A skirt of red wool is decorated with bands of the same material in black, sewn in horizontal stripes near the edge of the skirt. Over this is used the "mantelo" of black cloth and velvet, embroidered with jet. This is really a second skirt, bell-shaped, and worn over the first. The blouse is white with Swiss-type embroidery on the neck and cuffs. As a final adornment, a black and red shawl called a "dengue" covers the shoulders, crossed in front and tied at the back of the waist. A kerchief of bright colors edged in fringe covers the head.

In mountain regions, slight variations of this outfit exist. Streamers of colored ribbon may hang from the headdress, to be gathered in at the waist. Very often, native wooden clogs (resembling the Dutch) are worn instead of shoes.

The "maragato" dress is one of the most elegant in the region of Castile-León. A black cloth skirt is appliqued with embroideries of the same color. The shoulders are covered with a grand shawl of the kind known as "alfombrados," or carpeted, knotted at the back. The women of León braid their hair on the upper part of the heads, and on this great chignon rests a rich, natural silk kerchief of crimson tones. On the neck hang a great number of chains, necklaces, and rosaries, with marvelous trinkets enclosing relics.

The "maja" dress of Madrid has its origin in the eighteenth century. It consists of a bodice in velvet and satin, cut in pointed form on the skirt, with silk tassels and braids. On the head sits an ornament of tulle and lace and a bow which is called "Caramba," as it was first worn by a girl of that name.

The costumes of Mallorca and the Balearic Islands are time-honored replicas from this Mediterranean region. Silk skirts reach to the ground, worn with cotton aprons and black waists, and on the head "el rebocillo," of white lace and tulle, is fastened under the chin with a small fan in embroidered silk, called a "guadaret."

The costume of Navarra is known as "de roncalesa." It is rich and refined in nature, usually of dark cloth (blue), with a blouse embroidered in white and gold. The skirt is gathered up higher in front, allowing an underskirt of a lighter blue to be visible. The women's hair is combed into a long braid and secured by a bow of brocaded cloth.

The "charro" dress of Salamanca consists entirely of rich silk and gold embroideries. Hair is arranged in coils on both sides of the face and dressed with gold hairpins. The head is then covered with a white embroidered mantilla.

"La montera," a sort of bonnet, is typical of Segovia. It is made of a rich cloth, adorned with velvet and multi-colored ornaments. This is placed on a mantilla of white tulle. Embroidered aprons of black silk and velvet are worn over red and black velvet skirts.

Valencia presents vibrant color in the dresses of the women, made of damask-like cloth, silk and gold threads, with spangled aprons and shawls. The hair is fixed with combs, hairpins, and jewelry.

The people of Vasconia maintain their marine and rural traditions. The women's dress is extremely simple. The skirt is of red cloth, with outer edges fringed with black. Shoulders are covered with a shawl, and a white kerchief of triangular shape is worn on the head, tied in a manner peculiar to the area.

Zamora uses its handicraft of colored embroideries made without any previous design. The "gabacha" is an embroidered cloth covering the shoulders, the skirt, and the petticoat. Hair ribbons are also covered with this elaborate embroidery.

All dress is a product of ostentation; every phase of existence and every act of life requires distinct attire. Costumes conceived for dancing at celebrations and fiestas are more embellished than those of everyday wear. And climate must be a consideration in the choosing of fabrics and materials. In the cold northern regions of Spain, the men are dressed in thick trousers with warm vests over the linen shirts. Ample, colored waistbands or "fajas" are worn along with white woolen stockings or leggings and the open-style "alpargatas."

In the south, men wear short jackets that meet the waist, with a shirt and vest, and a scarf around the neck. Their wide-brimmed hat is the "sombrero cordobés." At one time, it was customary for the men to wear a small round velvet hat called "calañé," over a kerchief tied on the head. This unusual form is pictured in the drawings and engravings of Andalucian folk subjects by the nineteenth-century illustrator, Gustave Doré.

The dancer's apparel is the representation and the reconstruction of traditional modes that have been present in Spain for centuries. The theatrical costume attempts to capture an element of human experience; the contours and impressions of a forgotten time and place.

CHAPTER XV

AL-ANDALUS

From tears of remembrance, I know no surcease,
What madness to leave you, Fair al-Andalus!

Ibn Said Al-Maghribi

Andalucia is southern Spain. It is the Spain of Seville, Córdoba, Cádiz, Málaga, Almería, Huelva, Jaén, and Granada. It is the Spain of hot summers, warm winters, a land of fine architecture which comes from a past culture of rare aesthetics. Andalucia is a region which could be the natural home of people reared on the neighboring African continent, and here, for centuries, the Moors ruled at the time when they had reached the highest stage of their civilization.

Costumes in Andalucia vary from one district to the other. The most typical is the cotton dress of "volantes" (ruffles) and a small shawl (mantoncillo) covering the shoulders. The women's hair is knotted in a classic chignon and usually adorned with flowers. Strands of hair pressed flat into curls against the cheeks or forehead are called "caracoles" or snails.

The Andalucian bailaora handles both the "mantón de manila" (the Spanish shawl) and the "bata de cola" (the dancer's dress with a long train) with equal disdain. The shawl flutters and the flounces of the skirt swirl about in careless abandon and in perfect unison with the driving rhythms.

"Pericones" are the large fans traditionally used by the women for the dances "Caracoles" and "Guajiras." They are held aloft in the right hand and twirled with dexterous inward motions. The fan rotation corresponds to the contrasts in rhythm in that if the tempo is slow, the motion of the fan is quick. When dancing at a faster pace, the fan responds with slower action.

There are many descriptions of the folklore of Andalucia. It is the outgrowth of naturalness and utter lack of pretense. Even more, it has a refinement of taste marking every dance and song. "Andaluz" stems from the Arabic "al-Andalus" ("Land of the Vandals"), and the melancholy cadence of Arabic heritage runs through all the songs. But this strain never completely dominates. There is always an optimistic feeling, due, most likely, to the blazing sun, wide seas, and fertile earth, which leave their brand on the spirit of the "Andaluz."

Fandangos are popular songs and dances. They found favor with Christianized

Moors who performed them in Granada. "Verdiales" is a form of the "Fandango" of Málaga and takes its name from a rural district. Musically, this "Fandango" is ternary (grouped in threes). As a rhythm, it is continuous, and it can be danced and sung at the same time.

In Seville, the street dance called "Sevillanas" dates as far back as the sixteenth century. At one time, the Sevillanas were termed "Bíblicas," as the movements and narrative incorporated biblical symbols. The characteristic of African music known as a call-and-response technique is evident in the stanzas of the Sevillanas, as the singer calls the dancers in a metrical pattern that always remains the same. Years ago, there were eight or more "coplas" or verses, but now only the first four are performed to the accompaniment of guitars and castanets, and are known as "Corraleras." Most likely they originated in the "cortijos" or ranches around Seville. Lyrics are sentimental, often extolling the virtues of Seville, the Giralda, the Guadalquivir and Triana. Sevillanas are light and infectious, and artists of stature bring quicksilver turns, strength and profundity to the stately gaiety. The use of castanets in Sevillanas makes the dance a provincial statement and removes it from the realm of flamenco. (Castanets are absent in traditional flamenco, although they are played today in cabaret and on the concert stage to broaden and color flamenco interpretations.)

In May, or on the seventh Sunday after Easter, a procession to a shrine deep in the swampland of Las Marismas honors the Virgin, Nuestra Señora del Rocío (Our Lady of the Dew). Thousands of decorated two-wheeled carts called "carretas" converge at the holy grotto. After a field Mass, the Virgin is brought out of the chapel on a wooden float, and is carried to the village of Almonte, and back again. In the open air, make-shift stores serve the pilgrims, and the hiss of sizzling olive oil announces the Andalucian specialty, "churros," doughnuts, to be eaten with hot chocolate. Hundreds upon hundreds of people pay their respect to the statue, and gather to dance the "Sevillanas del Rocío," while hundreds more play drums, flutes, guitars, tambourines and castanets.

The best castanets are of "granadillo," the hard wood of the pomegranate tree, carefully seasoned and carved by hand. The word "castanet" comes from the Spanish "castaña," and suggests that castanets were also made of chestnut wood. Walnut, ebony, rosewood, and mahogany are frequently used. The four pieces of precisely sized wood are held together with an ordinary cord, which is placed on the thumbs and pulled taut. A roll of the castanets is called "carretilla." It is accomplished with the smallest finger of the right hand striking the castanet, and then beating it with the remaining fingers in order. To complete the pattern, one beat follows from the left hand without a break. The five staccato notes must be of equal length and strength. "Golpes" are steady beats of a one-two pattern alternating the left hand with the right. There is a difference in tone between the two castanets; the higher tone is for the right hand, and the deeper is for the left.

Castanet technique is divided between the "carretillas" (rolls) and the "golpes" (beats). Castanets are played with spontaneity, but never do they stray from the rhythm.

Antonio Triana followed the example of Maestro Otero in teaching the fundamental castanet exercises. Patterns are basic and easily adapt to all the dance rhythms of the classical and regional schools. The dancer responds to the slow or rapid tempo and adds the counterbeats according to the measure of his or her "oído" or musical ear.

The skill, speed and coordination required to accompany one's own dance movements are only achieved through diligent application. Thoughtful practice of the prescribed routines is rewarded by the technical mastery of the hypnotic trill of the instrument.

Castanets are often carried near the dancer's body, tucked into a shirt or bodice. Whether this improves the tone is uncertain. It is said that the dancer's personal essence can enter the wood. More likely the old custom began in order to protect the castanets from acquisitive fingers in the dressing room!

Castanets are depicted in the Cantigas de Santa María of the thirteenth century, and may originally have been Phoenician, as their colonies were dancing centers. As instruments, though, they did not gain popularity outside Spain and southern Italy.

We know that the Assyrians and Egyptians had perfected music far beyond the standard civilizations of their time. Archeologists have unearthed drums, cymbals, tambourines, and castanets at the sites of their ancient cities.

The Assyrians were a war-like nation and made instruments that could be strapped to their bodies. When they captured war prisoners who were musicians, they were not put to death. It seems that people in 3000 BC were practical.

Pliny, the Roman historian who lived between the years 23 and 79 AD, wrote a treatise on the fine arts, giving a realistic picture of Roman life in his time. He spoke of castanets, and described them as made of ivory and set with precious stones. It is probable that the Romans carried the small instruments home as souvenirs of their Iberian occupation.

The richness and volume of Spanish folk dances accompanied by castanets are unique in Europe. Traveling from one village in Spain to another, one finds a new variety of dance, tonalities and rhythms. In areas such as Andalucia, nearly everyone knows how to dance a little and play a little, from infant to elder, and every town has several versions of its own typical dance.

"La Murga" was a strolling band of comedic actors, street musicians, and farcical dancers who wandered the villages and the countryside in the early 1900s. They offered hilarious parodies of local color which were called "cachondeo," or buffoonery, by the Sevillanos. The humor and grace of Andalucia possess such warmth and artistic merit that even amateur rompings have within them the core of art and the potential for theater.

The technique of the "village" dance is basic and fundamental. There are steps called "panaderos," "jerezanas," "matalaraña," "pasada," and "careo," and there are movements which in classical ballet terminology are "rond de jambe," "pas de basque," and "sissonne." There are turns to the right and to the left ("vueltas"), and there are "vueltas quebradas" ("renverse" or backward turns) which require a limber torso.

The dancing academies of Seville had their secure place in aristocratic society. The schools of Manuel Otero and Angel Pericet must be recognized. Both gentlemen were true guardians of the great tradition of the classic Spanish dance, and the meticulous "entre-chat six" of their "bolero" dancers would stagger the imaginations of ballet dancers today.

"Los Seises" is performed before the high altar of the Cathedral of Seville during the last three days of the Carnival after the Fiesta of Corpus Christi, by twelve boys

CASTANETS

"Carretilla" (Roll):

right hand:

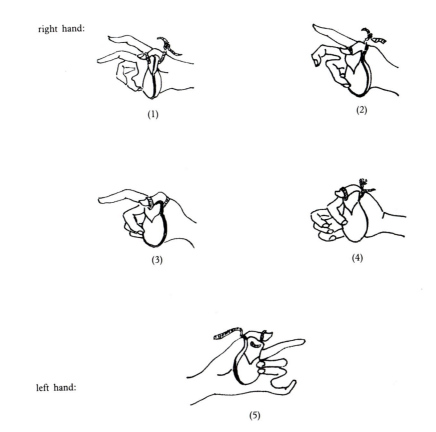

(1)

(2)

(3)

(4)

left hand:

(5)

from six to twelve years of age. They are dressed in the white and blue costumes of the time of Phillip II. It is said that this custom dates from the days when the children of Seville danced for joy when their town was at last delivered from the Moors.

At one period the Vatican forbade the continuance of this ceremony, but the prayers and protestations became so numerous that the Pope finally agreed that the dance could continue until the costumes wore out. . . . Needless to say, they are never allowed to wear out. Each year new material is added, and so the law is obeyed and the dance continues.

Andalucia developed a style of movement completely distinct from French-Italian, or even other Spanish regional influences. The Flamenco of Andalucia is without equal. In it, the male is manly, aggressive; the woman's role is prominent. The feet, the arms, the entire body are caught up in an emotional display. They tell of the Arab conquest, the psalms of David, and the immigration into Spain of the nomadic gypsy tribes.

In the year 525 BC, after the Egyptian Pharaoh was defeated by Cambyses, the successor of Cyrus and King of Persia, vanquished Egyptians fled into India. Some centuries later, they were scattered again by the Tartar invasion of the mighty conqueror Tamerlane. From Asia, these people roamed westward until they arrived in Spain in the fifteenth century.

Northern India is a region which has been subject to repeated racial invasions, and in which many racial mixtures are to be found. The dominant type, however, is the typical Hindu with the essential Mediterranean features. The swarthy people known today as Spanish gypsies have descended from the pariah or exiled tribes of India which wandered west to appear in Europe during the Middle Ages, and attached themselves to the Western peoples. Their ethnic mixture is Egyptian and Hindustani, and their racial type appears to be that of the Indian Mediterranean, although a mixture of Western blood is also present. Their speech and language have remained basically a modification of Sanskrit.

Musicologists look for the origin of the flamenco rhythms among the gypsies because the tribes were the most recent invaders of the Andalucian lands. Theorists who contend that flamenco is totally of gypsy invention disregard the fact that gypsies nowhere else but in Spain respond to the distinct rhythms in songs and dances. There is no flamenco style of movement among the Hungarian gypsies, the Rumanian "tziganos," or the Irish "connemaras." When the gypsies arrived in Spain, they may have danced "Villancicos," "Romances," and "Chaconas"; however, these dances had little in common with flamenco. Indeed, as Aben Hazem, the revered Cordovan philosopher insisted, flamenco rhythms are of Spanish origin, were indigenous in Andalucian culture, and were performed before the ninth century (date of the early Arabic musical archives). Of pure gypsy folklore, only three dances remain, the "Alboreá," "Cachucha" and "Mosca," and these are danced at their own private fiestas.

One hundred years ago, one had to cross the river from Seville to Triana over a bridge made of boats strung together on which planks were placed. The gypsies lived in Triana, tending their incandescent forges on Calle San Juan. Their center in Seville was the Alameda de Hércules (Hercules Promenade).

Throughout their wanderings, the gypsies made few innovations in dance styles. Instead, they seemed to have deliberately perpetuated and exaggerated the traditional movements and the established musical formulae in regions they inhabited. Spanish gypsies fashioned their style of flamenco out of elements already present in Andalucia.

It is recorded that Hindu dancers performed in the summer palaces at Cádiz for the royal Spanish court, and their highly formalized gesture language must have exerted some influence on what became the "Andalucian style."

As in the Flamenco, the Hindu dance makes use of the hand-clap (the Spanish "palma," the Hindu "tala"). It is an essential element in timing and rhythm. The Hindi "Jhaptal" is similar to the flamenco "Bulerías" in that the hand-claps are arranged in a two-three-two-three pattern. The Indian "Chautal" is marked in steady beats of twelve, as is the flamenco "Soleares" and the "Alegrías." The Hindu dance incorporates the use of finger cymbals made of metal or wood, and it is not unusual for primitive peoples to use hand instruments to accompany their dancing. In far-away Polynesia, small stones or beach pebbles known as "ili-ili" brush each other in the palms of the island dancers.

If we theorize that some of flamenco's restless rhythms were indeed brought by the gypsies across the Ganges and through the parched deserts, we must also remember that they took seed only in Spain. There was an affinity between the Phoenician, Semitic, Moorish, and Arabic legacy of the people who accepted these rhythms and allowed them to flourish and grow.

The temperament of the gypsy people, however, added a strong pungency to the existing "cante jondo" (deep song) which is completely Andalucian, and which cannot be imitated by anyone not raised in its traditions. The outstanding Spanish scholar, Felipe Pedrell, gathered a great number of the "cante jondo" melodies and published them in his invaluable "Cancionero." More important, he communicated much of his profound understanding of the roots of Spanish music to his gifted pupil, Manuel de Falla, who said, "El gitano con gracia es el gitano Andaluz." ("The gypsy with grace is the Andalucian gypsy.")

CHAPTER XVI

FOLKLORE

The South is a wasteland
Which weeps as it sings.

Luis Cernuda

Manuel de Falla (1876–1946) was born in Cádiz. His *El Amor Brujo* (Love Bewitched) is a choreographic fantasy or ballet directly based on gypsy material, as its subtitle, "'Gitanerías,'" indicates. With *El Amor Brujo*, the composer describes the life of gypsies in the caves of the Sacro-Monte of Granada. The ritual invocations and the "ghost" who possesses a being and breathes into it the obsession of desperation and death form the very base of the "cante jondo."

The plot is as follows:

The scene is a gypsy encampment. Legend tells the tale of Candelas who was betrothed to a wicked, cruel gypsy. In death, he mocks her as he did in life, and the fortune-teller's cards warn of eternal possession. She is not free to love the faithful Carmelo. In despair, Candelas and the gypsies draw a magic circle and while they mutter their incantations, she performs the Ritual Dance of Fire round a smoking cauldron. These efforts are in vain and the gypsies enlist the help of the girl Lucía. The dead lover's insistent theme weakens as he succumbs to her enticement. Carmelo convinces Candelas of his true love and the evil spell is broken forever.

The music, charged with the task of evoking the gypsy setting, naturally had to borrow the design of the "jondo" songs and the flamenco dances. We find a poignant "Polo" in an early scene in the shadowy cave. The first song echoes the "Soleá," the song of sorrow and loneliness. The "Danza del Terror" is inspired by a "Tanguillo" of Cádiz, as is the "'Danza del Fuego" itself. The "Fuego Fatuo" ("Will-o'-the-Wisp") is the rhythm of the rapid "Bulerías." The success of the ballet is due to the flavor of its gypsy-Moorish style, which is rich in drama, dissonances, and pulsating accents. To this, Falla added his own internal rhythm and his own profound human emotions.

Song: "Fuego Fatuo."–

Lo mismo que er fuego fatuo, lo mismito es er querré.
(Love is like capricious fire.)

Le juyes, y te persigue,
(You flee from it and it follows you,)
le yamas, y echa a corré. . . .
(you call it and it runs away. . . .)

The plot of Falla's *Sombrero de Tres Picos* (*Three-Cornered Hat*), on the other hand, bears no relation to the gloomy atmosphere that completely pervades *El Amor Brujo*. He is still in Andalucia, but an Andalucia characterized by the joy of life so vividly painted by Goya in his tapestry cartoons. Couples dance the "Seguidilla" to the strains of a guitar, to which the tambourine gives the rhythm. We picture a sunlit location, and Pablo Picasso actually created the light, witty landscape for the original production. The dances feature exciting solos and pas de deux, and a vigorous ensemble for a "Jota" finale. Boys wave capes before imaginary bulls, and straw effigies are tossed into the air. The characters of the ballet include a miller's pretty wife, the very jealous miller, a gouty Corregidor (governor of the town) in a three-cornered hat which is the sign of his lofty office, gossiping neighbors, a blackbird and a cuckoo, all having a thoroughly good time.

In order to steep himself in the feeling of the final Jota, Falla accepted an invitation from his friend, the famous painter, Ignacio Zuloaga, to spend some time in Aragón, and so it is that the real "Jota Aragonesa" resounds in the *Three-Cornered Hat*. Various folk themes are present in the ballet, including the playful nursery rhyme "San Serení." The "Miller's Dance" is based on the "Farruca" of Jerez. Cries of "¡Olé!" are uttered by dancers before the curtain even rises, and Falla included a song without accompaniment – an old children's roundelay, which differs from region to region in Spain. Some are of the opinion that it comes from Málaga, while others have claimed it for Seville. It is of country children singing:

Casadita, casadita, cierra con tranca la puerta;
(Little wife, little wife, bolt your door;)
que aunque el diablo esté dormido,
(even though the devil is sleeping,)
a lo mejor se despierta!
(he may awaken!)

Federico García Lorca (1898–1936), a major figure of world literature, was also a musician and composer. In Granada, where he lived as a youth, Lorca spent much time with the gypsies, studying their music and dance, writing poems in their caves, and learning their folktales. On top of the adjacent hill to Granada is the Alhambra, Spain's most impressive Moorish fortress, and the turbulence of the North African life-force and sensuality runs through Lorca's poetry and song.

In Madrid, in the 1920s, Lorca joined a circle of artists, modernists, and surrealists, including Salvador Dali, Luis Buñuel, and Rafael Alberti. Lorca's international reputation was won largely on the strength of his poetry, songs and ballads, which combine the passion and turmoil, the music, dance, and wonder which still continue, in spite of repressions, to seek existence. "The song is the soul of our souls," he said, "a lyric river bed through which pour all the aches and ritual expressions of our race."

Of an anguished horseman on his way to Córdoba, a destination he never reaches, Lorca wrote: "Córdoba, Lejana y sola." ("Córdoba, Distant and lonely.") He also resurrected a folk melody to which he wrote these verses:

Zorongo Gitano (Song and Dance)

Los zapatos que tú hacías,
(The shoes you made,)
zapatero de mi arma,
(shoemaker of my soul,)
son estrellas que relucen
(they are stars that shine)
alredor de mi enagua.
(around my petticoat.)

Estribillo
(Refrain)

La luna es un pozo chico.
(The moon is but a small well.)
Las flores no valen nada.
(The flowers are worth nothing.)
Lo que valen son tus brazos,
(What are of value are your arms,)
cuando de noche me abrazan.
(when they embrace me in the night.)

The waves of history that have swept over and dominated Spain left cultural traces which are expressed in all the traditional songs that accompany the grace and agility of the dancing.

Jota (Regional—Traditional)

Quien no dobla la rodilla
(He who does not kneel)
delante de una mujer
(before a woman)
ni ha conocido a su madre
(either has not known his mother)
ni sabe lo que es querer.
(or does not know what is love.)

Soleares (Flamenco—Traditional)

Me pesa el haberte hablao
la alegría de mi cara serrana
te las llevao.
(I am sorry I ever spoke to you.
There was happiness on my face,
but you stole it away.)

Siguiriya (Flamenco—Traditional)

Como las flores almendro
tienes tu la cara.
(Your face is like almond blossoms.)
Y la cintura,
y la cintura,
como junco de río
baña de agua.
(Your waist has the suppleness of river reeds.)

Serrana (Traditional)

Una cordera, una cordera
(A ewe, a ewe)
yo crié en mi rebaño
(that I raised in my herd)
Una cordera, una cordera
(A ewe, a ewe,)
y de tanto acariciarla
(and from petting her too much)
se volvió fiera.
(she became wild.)
Y las mujes (mujeres)
(And the women)
cuanto más se acarician,
(the more you caress them,)
fieras se vuelven. . . .
(the wilder they become. . . .)

Some of the more profound verses were created to be sung. Others, less pious in nature, were intended to be danced. The lyrics are direct accounts of everyday feelings, often dealing with love, persecution, and revenge. Verses composed by gypsies are usually more primitive and less sophisticated than those of the Andalucians.

Manuel Benítez Carrasco, a native of Granada, was born in the gypsy quarter known as Albaicín. His poetry is a celebration of sentiment and imagery. He is also known as a moving reciter of his works, which, for the most part, depict the flamenco way of life: the dance, the bulls; the "alegría" (joy) and the "pena" (sorrow) of Andalucia. The meter of his verses often matches the accentuations of the "compás" (rhythm and beat) of the flamenco guitar:

Uno, Dos, Y Tres (Por Alegrías)

Uno, dos, y tres . . .
(One, two, three . . .)
Uno, dos, y tres . . .
(One, two, three . . .)
Uno, dos, y tres,

(One, two, three,)
Tres banderilleros en el redondel....
(Three banderilleros in the ring....)

Poema de la Siguiriya
Con cinco golpes,
(With five strokes,)
con cinco puñaladas,
(with five stabs,)
contesta la siguiriya
(answers the siguiriya)
desde la guitarra.
(from the guitar.)

"El Cid"—Rodrigo Díaz de Vivar (1040–1099)—is a national hero of Spain famous for his exploits in the war against the Moors. An epic poem of "The Cid," written in the latter half of the twelfth century, exists today in fragments only, yet still contains 3,700 lines praising the chivalrous knight. Operas inspired by the Cid's adventures were written by Sacchini, Cornelius, and Massanet.

We do not know what relation there is between historical facts and the stories preserved in poetry and lore. The tale of the "Siete Bandidos de Écija" ("The Seven Bandits of Écija") parallels the early thirteenth-century legend of Robin Hood, who stole from the rich to give to the poor. In Andalucia, people still nurture their memory.

CHAPTER XVII

FLAMENCO

Dancers with no hips
Sob in the mirrors . . . .

Federico García Lorca

The flamenco guitar descends from the early string instruments present in Egypt and Babylonia and from the "laúd," brought into Spain by the Arabs. The Moors contributed their "khitras" or "khitarras," which were surely the ancestors of what today is the "guitarra."

The "guitarra morisca," an oval-shaped, three-stringed instrument, was in evidence when musicians from Mesopotamia established a school of Andalucian music in the city of Córdoba in the ninth century. The fourth and fifth strings were added by the time wandering minstrels of Toledo and Zaragosa accompanied their singing, and by the eighteenth century Padre Miguel García Basilio was writing "Fandangos" for a guitar of six strings.

The distinctive style of Andalucian guitarists was noted in early Spanish literature, and, at last, with the outset of the Café Cantantes (1840 on), professional flamenco guitarists were hired to play in these cafés. For the first time, singers and dancers from all regions of Andalucia gathered under one roof to perform.

Many flamenco singers do not know the names of musical notes, and so they will tell a guitarist to play "por el medio" ("in the middle" – the chord of A Major), or they will say "por arriba" ("upwards" – the chord of E Major). These instructions refer to positions on the fingerboard of the guitar.

The flamenco guitar, traditionally made of cypress, is a harmonic-percussive instrument incorporating the technique known as "rasgueado," or running the individual fingers of the right hand over the strings consecutively. This produces the strumming effect. The right thumb (pulgar) strikes the individual notes and "picado" is the plucking of the strings. "Ligados" are connected passages played with the left hand.

The impact of flamenco music is magnified when one considers that there is no written music for it. Each guitarist must learn all the rhythms and then polish them with his own style and creativity.

The mountains, Sierra Morena, form a barrier that separates Andalucia from the rest of Spain. The flamenco song, the Cante Jondo, developed in this natural isolation.

It recalls the song of the "muezzin" from the minarets signalling the faithful sons of Islam to prayer. An analogy also exists between the Cante Jondo and the Hebrew chants of the synagogue:

Petenera

Dónde vas, bella judia
(Where are you going, beautiful Jewess,)
tan compuesta y a deshora?
(so late and so made up?)
Voy en busca de Rebeco,
(I go looking for Rebeco,)
que está en la sinagoga....
(who is in the synagogue....)

There is also the influence of the Byzantine chants introduced in Spain's churches when Catholicism was still in primitive form, but a profound fatalism infects all the Cante Jondo.

The origin of the term Flamenco in reference to singing and dancing is obscure. Literally the word means Flemish, and some theorize that it was first applied to the soldiers who fought in Flanders or who were stationed there when it was a Spanish possession. Upon returning to their homeland, they must have seemed a wild lot when singing and carousing in the streets at night. People would shrug and say, "After all, they are Flamencos." Then again, the word may be an offshoot of the Arabic "felag-mengu," which denotes a peasant in flight. The dance form flamenco survives, both as a relic of the past and as a living experience.

In flamenco song and dance there are two main categories: Cante Grande and Cante Chico. In this context, we translate "grande" as meaning serious, and "chico" as not so serious.

In Cante Grande, there are the rhythms of "Soleares," "Siguiriyas" (named for "Seguidillas" but spelled differently in the Andalucian dialect), "Serranas," "Playeras," "Cañas," "Polos," and "Livianas." There are songs which do not require guitar accompaniment – "Deblas," "Tonás," "Martinetes," and "Saetas."

There are songs that are now danced; "Peteneras," "Tarantas," "Tientos," and there are songs that are never danced; "Cartageneras," "Fandangos Grandes," "Granaínas," "Media Granaínas," "Jaberas," and "Mineras."

In the Cante Chico, there are "Alboreás," "Alegrías" ("Rosas"), "Bulerías," "Cantiñas," "Caracoles," "Fandanguillos," "Guajiras," "Malagueñas," "Mirabrás," "Romeras," "Rondeñas," "Tangos," "Verdiales," and "Zambras."

There are also flamenco songs with a rural, village flavor: "Bamberas," "Caleseras," "Marianas," "Nanas" ("Lullabies"), "Palmares," and "Trilleras."

Three dances survive as pure Sevillian folklore: the "Garrotín," "Vito," and "Sevillanas."

The "Gitano" flamenco and the "Andaluz" flamenco are somehow distinct. The gypsy style is characterized by a carefree, exaggerated use of the rhythm, whereas the Andaluz reveals a deeper sensitivity, a profound humanity which adheres to the traditional restrictions of "pure" flamenco.

A typical flamenco ensemble is composed of "cantaores" (singers), "bailaores" (dancers), "tocaores" (guitarists), and "jaleadores" (who set the beat). Their "palmas" (hand-claps) are essential, for they maintain the solid rhythm of the "cuadro," or "scene," which animates and stimulates the singers and dancers.

"Braceo" refers to the placement of the arms in Spanish dance, which the women undulate in curved arched lines in their flamenco. Their wrists are supple, and their fingers curl sinuously. The men's arms are generally held in lower positions, with palms sloping downwards, but without twisting or rotating hands and fingers.

"Palmas," or handclaps, are accomplished as the right hand strikes the hollow in the palm of the left with the four fingers held together. For the muffled sound called "sordas," the hands are crossed with palm against palm beating in time, the fingers slightly open.

The resounding clicks of the "pitos," or finger snaps, are added in syncopation to the heelwork and further extend the rhythmic range. Both men and women excel at doing this with superb unconcern.

The cultural context of flamenco song and dance inherited much of its material from the Moors. Improvisation and the shouting of encouragement to the performers are elements deeply rooted in the African mystique.

The tide of Flamenco begins....

Alboreás—are songs and dances of gypsy wedding celebrations in the area of Sacro-Monte in Granada. They declare the purity of the bride-to-be.

Alegrías—both the song and the dance are of a festive nature, and originate, as does the "Mirabrás," from the cantinas of Cádiz. The rhythm came to Seville from El Puerto de Santa Maria. It is a demanding solo in the flamenco repertory, demonstrating the dancer's technical capabilities and ingenuity.

Guitarists and singers cannot always anticipate the dancers' flashes of invention or their sudden shifts of acceleration. They learn to respond to gestured signals. "Desplantes," and "llamadas," are distinctive heel-work combinations that summon changes in chords from the guitar and cue the singer's participation. This is particularly effective in the "Alegrías," where divisions of the dance are known as "entrada," "falseta," "castellana," "variación," and "ida."

Bulerías—is the combination of both song and dance in three-quarter rhythm and originated as "Jaleo de Jerez."

Farruca—is only accompanied by the guitar and the "palmas." It has more similarity to the northern dances found in the provinces of Galicia and Aragón. It is never sung, and it has borrowed its intrinsic flavor and elegance from the Andaluces.

Martinete—is old in tradition, but of poor melodic quality. The song accompanies the rhythm of primitive crafts that seem to have required musical assistance. The beat of the hammer (martillo) of the Andalucian blacksmith shops has given the name to the song. It is sung without guitar.

Petenera—alternates three-eighths and three-quarter rhythm. It has a quality somewhat detached from Andalucian folklore. Its origin may have been ancient Hebrew religious music; the chants of the Jewish synagogues in Spain. Another belief is that the Petenera was born in Paterna de la Ribera, Cádiz, and the name is the result of a change of the word "paterna." A tragic legend of the doomed singer who created the song adds to the mystery and magic spell of the rhythm.

Saeta – is an arrow, and the "ay" of mourning runs through this chant of suffering throughout all Andalucia. The song expresses the anguish of Christ on his march to Mount Calvary. It is therefore sung during the processions of Holy Thursday and Good Friday. There are Saetas for "Siguiriya" and Saetas for "Martinete," the latter being the most popular.

Siguiriya – came into being without the dance, possibly as a derivation of the old Andalucian melody called "Plañera." (Plañideras were professional mourners, women hired to wail and cry at funerals.) Whether these songs are referred to as "Siguiriya" or "Siguiriya Gitana," the prevailing theme is sorrow and lamentation. The dance is relatively modern. Siguiriya is the Andalucian term for the Castilian "Seguidilla," but the metric composition for the dance is not the same.

Serrana – is a lonely song of retreat. It is the "Caña" of the shepherds and smugglers of the mountains. According to Falla, these songs were of remorse for the repose of the souls of travelers robbed and murdered by mountain bandits.

Soleares – is primarily a song; the dance has gradually been added, as in the "Caña" (Arabic-"Gannia"). It is one of flamenco's oldest songs. Its steady beat and the infinite guitar variations which may be created for its tempo allow for movements of great beauty in the dance. It is, however, another song of "plañideras," sorrow and loneliness.

Tango – of Andalucia is a slow, majestic rhythm. In ancient times it may have had religious significance. It is older and more dramatic than the mischievous "Tanguillo," which stems from it. Sailors from the Andalucian ports who braved the seas with Columbus and Cortés hummed and made merry to the rhythms of Cádiz. (The reveille of the Spanish troops called "la deana" eventually became the general theme of the Mexican "Jarabe Tapatio.") Their Tanguillos in the New World became the "Veracruzanas" of Mexico, the Creole dances of the South, and the "Rumbas" of Cuba and Puerto Rico. "Rumba Flamenca" is this same Latin American Rumba with slight modifications.

Tarantas – are songs ("de Tarantos" is the dance) of the mining regions of Spain. Originating from the eastern seacoast, they have much in common with the "Cartageneras," the cantes de Levante from Cartagena.

Tientos – are dances accompanied by songs of the same rhythmic nature, unquestionably Arabic in ethnic origin.

Zambra – is also of Arabic origin, and the word "zambra" once meant moonlight. It was a favorite of the Moors as well, and they danced it during Easter Processions in Granada.

Zapateado – is a dance of creative impulse. Both the feet and the guitar become instruments of rhythm, and the upper body expresses purity of line. The Alegrías, Farruca, and Zapateado were the only dances performed by the men in the old "colmaos" or taverns. The women excelled in their own versions of the Alegrías, Bulerías, and Tangos.

The name "Antonio" is spoken with reverence by the flamencos, for the famous Antonio Ramírez, known as Ramirito, was born in Jerez in the late nineteenth century and performed his intricate "Farruca" in the Café Kursaal in Seville. Antonio Bilbao startled Andalucia with the swift "escobilla" (brisk, brush-like steps) of his "Zapateado." And there are the exceptional Sevillanos: Antonio Ruiz Soler, Antonio Montoya, who is the gypsy called "El Farruco," and Antonio Triana.

Traditional, authentic technique intermingles with contemporary ideas and meanings ... this is the message of the dance. But like the winding Guadalquivir River that follows its own tortuous course, Flamenco lives for the moment, with memories of yesterday and little thought of tomorrow.

Spanish dance treasures its past; the accumulated wisdom of the old songs; the native movement that ritualizes love, hope, domination and death; and the stark grief of flamenco that retraces the spiritual journey of mankind.

Antonio Triana spoke of this. The wistful boy who once pressed his face against a casement window to watch dancers turn and stamp never ceased to marvel at the darkling passion of his own Spanish soul, flaming into art and thunderous applause:

> **For many years now, I have had the desire to recapitulate the knowledge I've acquired in my long dancing career; above all, to find a way in theoretical form to explain and demonstrate in simple manner the various techniques of my dance, and perhaps arrive at a practical method of teaching this great choreographic art called the "Danza Española." This special school of dance, which I myself have helped to create, has as its base original principles of the traditional Spanish Dance. This cannot be reformed or modernized, for it would lose the savor of tradition. It can, however, admit contemporary sentiments and interpretations, changes of color and choreographic pattern, but it must never lose sight of its initial conception.**
>
> **The dances are, after all, unique creations of each Spanish province, reflecting the joy of the populace in their celebrations, their great internal rhythms, unequaled in any other country. Songs which have outlasted the centuries color this plasticity, which continues to merit the admiration of the entire world.**
>
> **I personally have had the pride of being one of the first dancers to have conveyed the mysterious rhythms of the Spanish Dance to foreign lands. I have been able to contemplate, again with pride and delight, the admiration with which we have been received abroad. Spain was once the "Mother Country" of the world, and perhaps that is why a Jota from Aragón is greeted with such enthusiasm everywhere. By way of contrast, the Zapateado of Cádiz receives an "Olé" from an audience in Canada worth more to the Spanish dancer than ten "Olés" echoing from a theatre in Seville. What magic has the phrase—Olé—from a cheering public as it crosses the footlights, causing an explosion of humility and dignity within the artist who hears it!**
>
> **I reaffirm that the Spanish Dance, descending to us from ancient roots, is the most interesting dance in the world, a free dance, frank and spontaneous, but at the same time faithfully guarding its past, as if to say, "DO NOT STRAY FROM THE PATH OF OUR ANCESTORS, OR IT WILL NO LONGER BE OUR DANCE!"**

From Antonio's notes in Spanish:

Años hace que en mi imaginación han habido deseos de recopilar los conocimientos adquiridos en mi larga carrera de bailarín; sobre todo, buscar la manera, en forma teórica, de explicar en sistema sencillo las diferentes técnicas y poder demostrar y quizás hacer llegar a la práctica, cierta escuela de este gran arte coreográfico llamado "Danza Española." Y cuya escuela especial, despues de larga experiencia, y creada por mí mismo, estará basada en los principios originales de la tradicional Danza Española, porque esta danza no puede ser reformada o modernizada, o dejaría de ser original, perdiendo el sabór de su tradicion. Sin embargo, admite cierta adición en color y forma coreográfica sin que pierda el sentido de su trascendencia original, creación única de cada provincia; y para regocijo de los pueblos de España en sus fiestas únicas, de una plasticidad sin igual y un gran ritmo interno, coloreado a veces por las canciónes que el pueblo transmitió por centurias, y que actualmente sigue deleite y encanto de admiración de todo el mundo.

Yo, personalmente, tengo el orgullo de ser de los primeros bailarines que han llevado a tierras lejanas el misterioso ritmo de las danzas de España de este siglo. He podido contemplar con cuanta admiración y deleite hemos sido acogidos tanto yo, como mis colaboradores o contemporáneos. Y a veces, me ha parecido a través de esa percepción de nuestras danzas por esos pueblos lejanos que España fuese la Madre Patria del mundo entero, con que entusiasmo recibían una Jota Aragonesa; o a manera de contraste, un Zapateado de Cádiz. Un "Olé" de un público en el Canadá vale por diez de un público de Sevilla. . . . Que misterioso tiene la frase – Olé-cuando sale del público y como transmite hasta que llega a generalizarse en forma apoteósica para orgullo del artista que la escucha.

Yo afirmo que la danza Española, de raíces antiquísimas, es la danza mas interesante del mundo, danza libre, franca y espontánea al mismo tiempo, pero fielmente guardada por nuestros antepasados, como diciendo, "NO TE SALGAS DE LA LÍNEA TRAZADA POR NUESTROS ABUELOS, O DEJARÍA DE SER NUESTRA DANZA!"

BIBLIOGRAPHY

Chase, Gilbert. *La Música de España.* Trans. Jaime Pahissa. Buenos Aires, Argentina: Libreria Hachette, S.A., n.d.

Craig, Gordon A. *Europe Since 1914.* 3rd ed. Hinsdale, Illinois: The Dryden Press, Inc., 1972.

Echague, José Ortiz. *España: Tipos y Trajes.* 7th ed. Bilbao, Spain: La Editorial Vizcaina, 1947.

Heaton, E. W. *Everyday Life in Old Testament Times.* New York: Macmillan Publishing Co., 1956.

Keay, Dr. Simon. *Roman Spain.* California: University of California Press, 1988.

Nettl, Bruno. *Folk and Traditional Music of the Western Continents.* New Jersey: Prentice-Hall, Inc., 1965.

Pohren, Donn E. *The Art of Flamenco.* Dorset, England: Musical Services Ltd. Guitar House, 1984.

Puig, Alfonso Claramunt. *Ballet y Baile Español.* Barcelona, Spain: Montaner y Simon, S.A., 1944.

Smith, Rex. *Biography of the Bulls.* New York: Rinehart & Company, Inc., 1957.

Sokol, Martin L. *The New York City Opera.* New York: Macmillan Publishing Co., Inc., 1981.

INDEX

Other titles in the Choreography and Dance Studies

This book is part of a series. The publisher will accept continuation orders which may be cancelled at any time and which provide for automatic billing and shipping of each title in the series upon publication. Please write for details.